# 2011

## Awards for Excellence
### WINNING PROJECTS

## Project Staff

**Gayle Berens**
Senior Vice President
Education and Advisory Group

**Theodore C. Thoerig**
Author

**Adrienne Schmitz**
Contributing Author

**Annie Finkenbinder-Best**
Contributing Author

**James A. Mulligan**
Managing Editor

**Laura Glassman**
Publications Professionals LLC
Manuscript Editor

**Betsy VanBuskirk**
Creative Director

**Craig Chapman**
Senior Director, Publishing Operations

## Design and Composition

InterCommunicationsInc
Newport Beach, California
www.intercommunications.com

Urban Land Institute
1025 Thomas Jefferson Street, NW
Suite 500 West
Washington, DC 20007-5201

**Recommended bibliographic listing:**
Thoerig, Theodore C. *Awards for Excellence: 2011 Winning Projects*. Washington, D.C.: Urban Land Institute, 2011.

ISBN-978-0-87420-166-6
ULI Catalog number: A29

## About the Urban Land Institute

The mission of the Urban Land Institute is to provide leadership in the responsible use of land and in creating and sustaining thriving communities worldwide. ULI is committed to

- Bringing together leaders from across the fields of real estate and land use policy to exchange best practices and serve community needs;
- Fostering collaboration within and beyond ULI's membership through mentoring, dialogue, and problem solving;
- Exploring issues of urbanization, conservation, regeneration, land use, capital formation, and sustainable development;
- Advancing land use policies and design practices that respect the uniqueness of both built and natural environments;
- Sharing knowledge through education, applied research, publishing, and electronic media; and
- Sustaining a diverse global network of local practice and advisory efforts that address current and future challenges.

Established in 1936, the Institute today has nearly 30,000 members in over 90 countries, representing the entire spectrum of the land use and development disciplines. ULI relies heavily on the experience of its members. It is through member involvement and information resources that ULI has been able to set standards of excellence in development practice. The Institute has long been recognized as one of the world's most respected and widely quoted sources of objective information on urban planning, growth, and development.

**A guiding principle** of the Urban Land Institute is that the achievement of excellence in land use practice should be recognized and rewarded. Since 1979, ULI has honored outstanding development projects in both the private and public sectors with the ULI Awards for Excellence program, which today is widely recognized as the development community's most prestigious awards program. ULI Awards for Excellence recognize the full development process of a project, not just its architecture or design—although these elements play an important role in the overall project. Each award is presented to the development project, with the developer accepting on behalf of the project.

Nominations are open to all, not just ULI members. Juries of ULI full members, chaired by trustees, choose finalists and winners. Jury members represent many fields of real estate development expertise, including finance, land planning, development, public affairs, design, and other professional services. They also represent a broad geographic diversity.

ULI began the Awards for Excellence program in 1979 with the objective of recognizing truly superior development efforts. The criteria for the awards involve factors that go beyond good design, including leadership, contribution to the community, innovations, public/private partnership, environmental protection and enhancement, response to societal needs, and financial success. Winning projects represent the highest standards of achievement in the development industry, standards that ULI members hold worthy of attainment in their professional endeavors. All types of projects have been recognized for their excellence, including office, residential, recreational, urban/mixed use, industrial/office park, commercial/retail, new community, rehabilitation, public, and heritage projects, as well as programs and projects that do not fit into any of these product categories.

For the first three years of the program, only one Award for Excellence was granted each year. In 1982, ULI trustees authorized awards for two winners—one large-scale project and one small-scale project—to recognize excellence regardless of size. Starting in 1985, the awards program shifted emphasis to product categories, while also retaining the small- and large-scale designations. As the program matured, new categories were added to reflect changes in the development industry. In 2002, the last year in which winners were awarded by category, there were 18 categories and up to 11 possible awards.

The Special Award was established in 1986 to acknowledge up to two projects and/or programs that are socially desirable but do not necessarily meet the official awards guidelines governing financial viability and exemplary projects that are not easily categorized. In 1989, the Heritage Award was introduced to acknowledge projects that have established an industry standard for excellence and that have been completed for at least 25 years. As of 2011, only ten Heritage Awards have been granted.

When the awards program began, only projects located in the United States or Canada were considered. Beginning with the 1994 awards, ULI's board of trustees authorized the creation of an International Award for a project outside the United States and Canada. With the 2001 awards, the board eliminated this category, opening all categories to all projects, regardless of location.

In 2003, ULI eliminated all category designations, with the exception of the Heritage Award, and did more to recognize the excellence of all the finalist projects in the awards process, not just the award winners. In 2004, ULI inaugurated the ULI Awards for Excellence: Europe, Middle East, and Africa (EMEA, formerly Europe), adopting the same criteria and a similar selection process, and juried by EMEA-based ULI members. And in 2005, the Awards for Excellence program continued to evolve with the introduction of the ULI Awards for Excellence: Asia Pacific.

Also new in 2005 was the introduction of the ULI Global Awards for Excellence. A select jury of international members, charged with choosing up to five Global Award winners from among that year's 20 award-winning projects, announced three global winners in 2005. In each year since, five projects have won Global Awards.

The 2012 "Call for Entries" for the Awards for Excellence competitions is now available on the ULI Awards web page (www.uli.org/uliawards).

## JUDGING CRITERIA

1. Although architectural excellence is certainly a factor, the ULI Awards for Excellence is not a "beauty contest."
2. The project or program must be substantially completed. If the project is phased, the first phase must be completed and operationally stable.
3. No specific age or time constraints apply, except for the Heritage Award (which recognizes projects and/or programs that have been completed for at least 25 years).
4. The project must be financially viable, which means it must be in stable operation and financially successful. An applicant must be able to document the prudent use of financial resources to justify the achievement of a financial return. Programs and projects developed by nonprofit or public agencies are necessarily exempt from the financial viability requirement.
5. The project must demonstrate relevance to the contemporary and future needs of the community in which it is located. The community reaction to the project also is taken into consideration.
6. The project must stand out from others in its category.
7. The project must be an exemplary representative of good development and a model for similar projects worldwide.

## SELECTION PROCESS

1. Applications are available as a downloadable document on the ULI website's Awards page (www.uli.org/uliawards) on December 1.
2. Developers and/or other members of the development team submit completed applications to ULI by a given date in February. Each completed entry must contain the developer's name and signature.
3. The Awards for Excellence jury convenes to review submissions and choose finalists.
4. At least one jury member visits each finalist project.
5. When all site visits have been completed, the jury reconvenes to evaluate the finalist projects and choose award winners. Among all regions, the jury may also choose one Heritage Award winner.
6. The award winners are announced and honored at ULI's Fall Meeting.

# CONTENTS

# *Global* WINNERS

## DEVELOPMENT TEAM

**Developer/Owner**
*Ed Roberts Campus*
*Berkeley, California*
*www.edrobertscampus.org*

**Development Manager**
*Equity Community Builders*
*San Francisco, California*
*www.ecbsf.com*

**Architect**
*Leddy Maytum Stacy Architects*
*San Francisco, California*
*http://lmsarch.com*

## *Jury* STATEMENT

Conceived by a consortium of partners committed to serving people with disabilities, Ed Roberts Campus is an international center for the Independent Living Movement in Berkeley, California. The 1.6-acre, 65,000-square-foot facility was constructed using universal design principles and provides mutually supportive office space, a child care center, and direct access to a Bay Area Rapid Transit station.

# ED ROBERTS CAMPUS, Berkeley, California

Named for a prominent Bay Area disability activist, the Ed Roberts Campus in Berkeley, California, is the satisfying product of a long and laborious effort by local activists and nonprofits.

Conceived by a consortium of like-minded partners committed to serving people with disabilities, the facility has become an international center for the Independent Living Movement and a community center that improves links to public transportation and celebrates diversity. The 1.6-acre (0.65-ha), 65,000 square-foot (6,039-m²) facility was constructed using universal design principles and provides mutually supportive office space, a child care center, and direct access to a Bay Area Rapid Transit (BART) station.

In 1998, seven organizations—each sharing a common history in the Independent Living Movement—joined to plan and develop a socially equitable and environmentally sustainable campus. The concept of the campus took form shortly after the death of Edward V. Roberts— an early leader in the movement to enable all persons with disabilities to fully participate in society and one of the first people with disabilities to attend the University of California, Berkeley—as a way to commemorate his life and contributions. Civic leaders and disability activists felt that supporting the organizations that Roberts helped flourish would be the best and most enduring way to honor his work.

The design process spanned five years and involved intensive community engagement with neighbors, merchants, and the historic preservation community of south Berkeley. The Ed Roberts Campus member organizations hired Equity Community Builders as development manager and Leddy Maytum Stacy Architects to lead the design team, with initial grant funds from the city and private foundations. Ultimately, the development was financed through a mix of public grants, private foundation money, and new market tax credits. The development and design teams held extensive discussions with residential neighbors adjacent to the site, many of whom were deeply concerned about the scale of the building.

The campus, sited on a former BART parking lot, includes exhibition space, community meeting rooms, a child care center for children with disabilities, a fitness center, offices, vocational training facilities, and a café organized around an enclosed courtyard. A subgrade

garage provides parking, and an underground walkway connects the project with the adjacent Ashby BART station. Local citizens were initially concerned about the height and mass of the building; however, the arcing transparent facade with slatted wood screens presents a soft and approachable face to the building. Where the campus faces single-family residents, the building steps back at the second floor, reducing its presence on the street and allowing outdoor terraces. A sloping steel fascia spans the main facade, framing the public plaza and rising to the south at the building's most prominent and busiest corner.

The red helical ramp, at the center of the lobby, is the central design feature at the Ed Roberts Campus. Instead of a traditional switchback ADA-compliant ramp, Bay Area–based Leddy Maytum Stacy Architects designed the spiral ramp, which has a diameter of 56 feet (17 m), to allow both able-bodied people and people with disabilities equal access to the floors above. Other thoughtful design elements reinforce the equitable ethos of the campus: doors sense a user's approach, pebbled walkways and a splashing fountain serve as wayfinding devices for sight-impaired visitors, and secured-access readers can read security cards from a few feet away for those who cannot use their arms.

## PROJECT DATA

**Web Site**
*www.edrobertscampus.org*

**Site Area**
*1.6 ac (0.65 ha)*

**Facilities**
*65,530 sf (6,088 m²) office*
*17,621 sf (1,637 m²) open space*

**Land Use**
*office, restaurant, open space*

**Start/Completion Dates**
*August 2008–November 2010*

The Ed Roberts Campus is a powerful and attractive example of the efficacy of universal design. The logical design elements used throughout prove that, with ingenuity, both form and function can be achieved when designing for all users. As John King, urban design critic for the *San Francisco Chronicle* commended: "The existence of this campus does more than honor a pioneer. It is an egalitarian oasis that, with luck, will send ripples into the mainstream."

## DEVELOPMENT TEAM

**Owner/Developer**
*New World Symphony*
*Miami Beach, Florida*
*www.nws.edu*

**Design Architect (Building)**
*Gehry Partners, LLP*
*Los Angeles, California*
*www.foga.com*

**Design Architect (Park)**
*West 8 Urban Design and*
*Landscape Architecture*
*B.V. Rotterdam, The Netherlands*
*www.west8.nl*

## Jury STATEMENT

The New World Center is an innovative facility for classical music education and performance in Miami Beach, Florida, that sits at the intersection of architecture, technology, education, and culture. An 80-foot-high glass-and-steel box contains the free-flowing theater space, while the front facade—which doubles as a 7,000-square-foot projection wall—displays concerts and video art to patrons in an adjacent 2.5-acre green space.

# NEW WORLD CENTER, Miami Beach, Florida

The New World Center has helped usher in a new development model, turning the traditional concert hall—with its orderly rows and grand décor—inside out.

Establishing new connections among architecture, technology, education, and culture, the Frank Gehry–designed glass-and-steel box contains the free-flowing theater space, while the front facade doubles as a 7,000-square-foot (650-m²) projection wall, displaying concerts and video art to patrons in an adjacent 2.5-acre (one-ha) urban park. Known as the Miami Beach Soundscape, this outdoor venue brings classical music and performance to an audience beyond the formal environs of most symphony halls.

By the late 1990s, the New World Symphony (NWS) was outgrowing its first home, the Lincoln Theater, whose renovation two decades earlier had been central to the revival of Lincoln Road in Miami Beach. At the height of the real estate boom in 2008, the city gave NWS two large empty parcels for its new home that were used at the time for service parking. That magnanimous gesture—those were the last two developable parcels in Miami Beach—and $45 million in public funds from the city kick-started the development that would ultimately lead to one of the most technologically advanced musical institutions in the world.

At the same time, Michael Tilson Thomas, world-renowned pianist and founder of the NWS, secured the architectural services of an old friend—Frank Gehry. The collaboration lent instant credibility to the venture, and in partnership with the city, the project grew to include a new urban open space and city parking garage. The initial $45 million in city funds was quickly leveraged to secure $141 million in private philanthropy, expanding the scope of the concert hall.

The New World Center not only turns the traditional concert hall inside out, but it also represents an inversion of Gehry architecture. The exterior is restrained, all straight lines and traditional glass-and-stucco facades. The interior, however, is signature Gehry: flowing, asymmetrical forms abound, with sail-like structures framing the atrium and performance space. The new urban park, designed by Dutch firm West 8, features sinuous paths and mature trees along with an open lawn that faces the projection wall. A towering glass wall

exposes the lobby, staircases, and rehearsal rooms, further connecting the public with the performers.

The 756-seat flexible performance hall is designed to break down the distance between the performances and the audience. Fourteen broad sail-like panels can project images or video, allowing further integration of aural and visual art. Many of the seats are retractable, so the room can convert into a single open space; the stage itself can be raised and lowered, to distinguish certain performers. The various configurations allow the NWS to experiment with different types of performances: from traditional symphonic performances to video-music collaborations, from half-hour $2.50 miniconcerts to traditional South Beach dance parties.

The new rehearsal and performance space houses the NWS, a quasi–finishing school that prepares musicians for future careers as members of orchestras and ensembles around the world. The campus enjoys access to Internet2—a system restricted to universities and thus unencumbered by commercial traffic—that carries real-time, high-definition videos throughout the building, allowing musicians to speak and play for conductors and composers throughout the world. A next-generation projector plays live concerts in crystal-clear detail on the outdoor wall, and a 67-speaker array relays music with surprising clarity and depth throughout the park. The enhanced technology allows greater access and potential for the NWS to reach colleagues and the public.

## PROJECT DATA

**Web Site**
*www.newworldcenter.com*

**Site Area**
*3.75 ac (1.52 ha)*

**Facilities**
*106,000 sf (9,849 m²) education and performance space*
*38,784 sf (3,603 m²) open space*
*550 parking spaces*

**Land Use**
*civic, education, open space*

**Start/Completion Dates**
*January 2008–November 2010*

PHOTOGRAPHY BY CLAUDIA URIBE (8)
CLAUDIA URIBE (10), RUI DIAS-AIDOS (10)
TOMAS LOEWY (11)

The New World Center is the centerpiece of a 15-year effort to rejuvenate the area of Miami Beach between the pedestrian shopping stretch of Lincoln Road and the convention center. But it also is an effort to rejuvenate the perception of classical music, which has for decades suffered from a stodgy, elitist image. As Thomas told the *Miami Herald*: "Everything about this building is new—the spaces, the way they work, the way they relate to the audience, the presence of the concerts on the skin of the building." In building the New World Center, the NWS hopes to start a new, more open dialogue among music lovers in Miami Beach.

The irregular facade is a jumble of bay windows and balconies, reducing the perceived mass of the 50-story towers. Almost the entire building (85 percent) used modular construction, facilitating the construction process in the tight, central-city site.

The sky bridges at the Pinnacle@Duxton have redefined the potential of a building feature that had fallen out of favor in urban design circles. For years, designers and developers criticized the sky bridge for pulling pedestrians off the sidewalks and deterring retail and pedestrian activity at street level. At the Pinnacle@Duxton, sky bridges have been recast as active destinations rather than passive thoroughfares. The sky gardens, with nearly two hectares (five ac) of open space, connect the seven buildings at two levels: the 26th story, which includes recreational facilities such as an outdoor gym, clubhouse, and full jogging track; and the 50th story, along the roofline, which is more contemplative and passive in activity and design, with seating areas, pavilions, and viewing platforms that create an "outdoor living room." An elevated open space caps the 1,088-space parking garage and flows down to street level, providing a seamless connection to the adjacent park and urban network.

The units at Pinnacle@Duxton are designed with a compact, rectilinear floor plan, free of columns, challenging the notion that affordable living in the city means congested and crowded spaces. The open floor plans, along with extensive recreational and family-friendly amenities—the development includes a kindergarten, a child care center, and two activity centers—are intended to attract young professionals and families.

## PROJECT DATA

**Web Site**
*www.pinnacleduxton.com.sg*

**Site Area**
*2.5 ha (6.2 ac)*

**Facilities**
*1,848 multifamily units
1,429 m² (15,382 sf) education space
793 m² (8,536 sf) retail and restaurant space
325 m² (3,498 sf) civic space
1,088 parking spaces*

**Land Use**
*residential, parks/open space, retail, education, civic*

**Start/Completion Dates**
*April 2005–December 2009*

The Pinnacle@Duxton reflects the ceaseless life cycle of the redevelopment of public housing in Singapore. Returning to the site of the HDB's first project, which was built to ease a national affordable-housing crisis, it illustrates the level of excellence that Singapore's national housing authority has reached. The interconnected high-density development redefines what high-rise living can be with its sky gardens and open spaces, breathes new life into an area of aging households, and provides affordable housing options in a central location. The building has become a point of national pride, winning numerous awards, including the Best Tall Building 2010 award from the Chicago-based Council on Tall Buildings and Urban Habitat.

PHOTOGRAPHY BY ARC STUDIO (12), HDB (14), HDB (14) ARC STUDIO (15)

## DEVELOPMENT TEAM

**Owners/Developers**
*Forest City Enterprises*
*Cleveland, Ohio*
*www.forestcity.net*

*Westfield Group*
*Sydney, Australia*
*www.westfield.com*

**Executive Architect**
*ka, Inc.*
*Cleveland, Ohio*
*www.kainc.com*

**Design Architect**
*RTKL Associates, Inc.*
*Baltimore, Maryland*
*www.rtkl.com*

**Associate Architects**
*Kohn Pedersen Fox Associates*
*New York, New York*
*www.kpf.com*

*Westfield Design*
*Sydney, Australia*
*www.westfield.com*

# WESTFIELD SAN FRANCISCO CENTRE, San Francisco, California

The 1.5 million-square-foot (139,355-m²) Westfield San Francisco Centre, one of the nation's largest urban shopping malls, comprises more than 170 specialty stores; two anchor department stores, Bloomingdale's and Nordstrom; four floors of Class A office space; a gourmet marketplace; and a nine-screen cinema. The $460 million expansion project restores the 1890s-era Emporium Building to its original grandeur and re-creates what a century ago was San Francisco's premier retail street.

Westfield San Francisco Centre integrates the adjacent San Francisco Shopping Centre, tripling the leasable area of the retail and entertainment complex.

Opened in 1896 as the West Coast's first full-service department store, the historic Emporium Building was once the hub of San Francisco's retail industry. Partially destroyed in the fires after the 1906 San Francisco earthquake, the beaux arts–style building reopened in 1908 and operated as a shopping destination for nearly another century. By the 1950s, however, residents began moving to and shopping in the suburbs, and the Emporium and Market Street area endured a steady decline. In the ensuing decades, the Emporium changed ownership multiple times before finally closing in 1996, leaving a hulking void in the retail district.

The redevelopment began with a partnership between two out-of-town developers: the Westfield Group—an Australian company that operates 119 shopping centers in the United States, Australia, New Zealand, and the United Kingdom—and Forest City Enterprises, a Cleveland-based development firm. Westfield purchased the existing shopping center in 1996 and partnered with Forest City to renovate and incorporate the historic Emporium Building. After protracted discussions with preservationists, two major architectural features of the original Emporium Building, designed by San Francisco architect Albert Pissis, were

## Jury STATEMENT

After an eight-year development process, Westfield San Francisco Centre has restored the city's historic Emporium building, boasting 1.5 million square feet of commercial space and attracting an estimated 25 million visitors to this once-distressed area of San Francisco.

## PROJECT DATA

**Web Site**
*www.westfield.com/sanfrancisco*

**Site Area**
*6.4 ac (2.6 ha)*

**Facilities**
*1,251,000 sf (116,222 m²) retail*
*249,000 sf (23,133 m²) office*

**Land Uses**
*retail, office, restaurant, entertainment, education*

**Start/Completion Dates**
*November 2003–September 2006*

saved and restored. The glass-and-steel dome 102 feet (31 m) wide—the 19th-century building's trademark feature, with its lunette windows, ornamental plasterwork, and galvanized metal frame—was painstakingly refurbished. Two large roof skylights frame the dome and illuminate the atrium, which rises 200 feet (61 m), and the colonnade below, affording views of the dome from all eight floors of the restored building. The developers also restored the beaux arts sandstone facade that fronts on Market Street—the only part of the building that withstood the 1906 earthquake and fire—to its original appearance, preserving the display windows, bronze doors, and even two old Emporium signs that flank the Market Street entrance.

Westfield San Francisco Centre expands the San Francisco Shopping Centre, which opened in 1988, connecting with the existing mall at five levels and creating a continuous retail and entertainment complex. The new section contains a 338,550-square-foot (31,452-m²) Bloomingdale's, the second largest in the country; a nine-screen movie theater; a 16,000-square-foot (1,486-m²) day spa; and seven full-service restaurants.

The upper four stories contain 249,000 square feet (23,133 m²) of Class A office space overlooking the atrium: nearly half the space is leased to San Francisco State University's MBA program, and the remaining area includes Microsoft's northern California offices. With no new parking included in the expansion, the developers connected the concourse level directly to the Bay Area Rapid Transit and Muni Metro stations at Powell Street to facilitate the use of public transit.

The design team included RTKL, which served as the design architect for the retail environment, entertainment zones, office space, and the historic fabric, including restoration of the Market Street facade and monumental dome; ka, Inc., which served as the executive architect and was responsible for preparing all construction documents and coordinating the effort; and Kohn Pedersen Fox Associates, which was the design architect for the core, shell, and contemporary, all-glass exterior of Bloomingdale's.

More than 95 percent leased and occupied, Westfield San Francisco Centre has generated $17.5 million in property and sales taxes for the city, created approximately 3,000 new jobs, and drawn more than 25 million visitors per year to the previously underused Market Street area. Among the 172 retailers, almost 47 percent are new to San Francisco, and preexisting San Francisco Shopping Centre tenants are reporting a 10 to 15 percent increase in sales since the reopening. After an eight-year development process, Westfield San Francisco Centre has become an economic engine for downtown San Francisco, creating connections with nearby Union Square, the city's established shopping district, and Yerba Buena, a cultural and entertainment area.

PHOTOGRAPHY BY DAVID WHITCOMB
(ALL IMAGES)

## DEVELOPMENT TEAM

**Developer**
*Places for People*
*London, United Kingdom*
*www.placesforpeople.co.uk*

**Design Architect**
*RPS Group*
*Abingdon, United Kingdom*
*www.rpsgroup.com*

## *Jury* STATEMENT

This historic former railway just outside Milton Keynes has been redeveloped to provide 300 mixed-tenure homes, alongside commercial space, community facilities, and a 2.5-acre park. Three Grade II listed buildings stand alongside two new buildings that complement each other well and provide a variety of housing solutions for the local community.

# WOLVERTON PARK, Milton Keynes,

**United Kingdom** On the site of a former railroad engineering works and popular recreational facility, Wolverton Park, a mixed-use community with an array of building types that acknowledges the area's history, has quickly become one of the most desirable places to live and work in Milton Keynes.

Wolverton Park has been completely transformed through a carefully calibrated mix of housing, commercial space, history, and deep community involvement.

The 4.25-ha (10.5-ac) site has 300 mixed-income housing units, 2,787 square meters (30,000 sf) of commercial space, and one hectare (2.5 ac) of open space. All of these new uses are woven into Wolverton Park's original facilities through cutting-edge design. A number of Victorian-era industrial buildings on site, including three that were designated as historically significant structures, were in an advanced state of disrepair, including an aging canal that has been restored as an important on-site amenity.

From these dilapidated structures, the developer, London-based Places for People, built housing units using the existing materials. One, the Triangle Building, was left with only a brick shell and the steel-and-brick roof supports. These housing units have been built around the original walls and match the original layout of the mechanical sheds the building originally housed. In the Royal Train Shed—which until 1991 housed the official train of Britain's royal family—the original columns and beams were restored, and the rails and crane used to lift railroad cars for repair have become key features of the entrance and access corridors of the attached townhome units. New materials used in construction, including red brick, glass, and stainless steel, were chosen to complement the existing buildings. The office and commercial space was fashioned from an old carriage works building, with a restaurant or pub set to occupy a historic spot that was once used as a break room by rail workers.

The designer, RPS Group, took care to thoughtfully consider input from the surrounding residents. The site had long served as a community facility for sporting events, with an athletics stadium, bowling green, and cycling track opened in 1885 as a recreational area for the rail yard workers and their families. Although many of the structures were no longer

in good repair, a replica was constructed of the grandstands surrounding the stadium and portions of the cycling tracks that circled the park in response to local interest.

Wolverton Park has emphasized sustainability through attention to transportation options and efficient buildings. All of the new construction, including that incorporating elements of the historic buildings, has an Eco-Homes "very good" standard, equivalent to a LEED (Leadership in Energy and Environmental Design) Platinum designation. Custom-designed solar panels are built on many of the units, and a train station is ready to transport passengers to London in just under an hour, reducing energy and transportation costs to residents.

Social sustainability is also an important and special feature of Wolverton Park. Places for People, the project developer, is a registered provider of affordable housing and was able to provide a number of financing mechanisms that acknowledge the current state of the market while encouraging both homeownership and rentals. The developer provides mortgage finance for buyers and is able to offer ownership opportunities to potential homeowners with a wide range of incomes, providing a full range of intermediate and lease-to-own financing structures. Because it is also responsible for community management, People for Places is invested in offering total "life cycle" community services, including preschool, business start-up advice, and elder care facilities.

## PROJECT DATA

**Web Site**
*www.wolverton-park.co.uk*

**Site Area**
*4.25 ha (10.5 ac)*

**Facilities**
*1,858 m² (20,000 sf) office space*
*929 m² (10,000 sf) retail space*
*300 multifamily units*
*432 parking spaces*

**Land Use**
*residential, office, retail, open space*

**Start/Completion Dates**
*January 2006–September 2009*

Through close partnership with institutional and community stakeholders—including Network Rail, the site's original owners, the British Waterways Board, local governments, and neighborhood groups and associations—Wolverton Park has become an integral part of the Milton Keynes community. Through thoughtful design and innovative community management, this long-disused railroad yard has been transformed into a vibrant place to live and work.

# Commercial | WINNERS

## DEVELOPMENT TEAM

**Developer**
*Hines Interests*
*Houston, Texas*
*www.hines.com*

**Owner**
*KBS REIT II, Inc.*
*Newport Beach, California*
*www.kbs-cmg.com*

**Design Architect**
*Pickard Chilton*
*New Haven, Connecticut*
*www.pickardchilton.com*

**Architect of Record**
*Kendall/Heaton Associates, Inc.*
*Houston, Texas*
*www.kendall-heaton.com*

## *Jury* STATEMENT

300 North LaSalle is a
60-story, 1.3 million-
square-foot office tower
on the north bank of the
Chicago River. The LEED-
Gold building maximizes
daylighting and minimizes
solar gain, uses river water
for cooling, and features
a half-acre plaza that
has helped activate the
riverfront.

# 300 NORTH LASALLE, Chicago, Illinois

The "City of the Big Shoulders," with its grid of broad streets and large skyscrapers, has added a 60-story high rise along the north shore of the Chicago River. Rising 800 feet (244 m), 300 North LaSalle, among the city's tallest buildings, offers 200 feet (61 m) of frontage along the river, featuring an outdoor plaza with seating and a large waterfront café.

Developed by Hines and designed by the architecture firm Pickard Chilton, the building continues the tradition of exceptional Chicago architecture. It also follows the more recent Chicago trend of sustainability. Jon Pickard, of Pickard Chilton notes, "Our design for 300 North LaSalle acknowledges the great tradition of the Chicago skyscraper, while redefining it for the 21st century." The project is certified LEED-CS (Leadership in Energy and Environmental Design for Core and Shell) Gold and earned the Energy Star designation from the U.S. Environmental Protection Agency.

The project occupies a 1.2-acre (0.5-ha) site. It includes 1.3 million square feet (120,774 m²) of office space, 15,000 square feet (1,394 m²) of shops and restaurants, three levels of underground parking, and public spaces—including a half-acre (0.2-ha) sunlit waterfront garden with access to the river. Major tenants include Kirkland & Ellis, LLP, Chicago's largest law firm; Boston Consulting Group; Quarles & Brady LLP; Aviva; and GTCR Golder Rauner, an insurance group.

Kirkland & Ellis signed on as the anchor tenant in 2005, and representatives for the firm participated in the strategic planning and site selection process. After evaluating multiple workplace scenarios, they defined the ideal building size and floor plate, and then selected Hines. The developer acquired the site and broke ground in 2006, completing construction in 2009.

One of the city's tallest buildings, 300 North LaSalle is designed to maximize perimeter offices, a plus for drawing high-profile tenants. The public space enhances the streetscape and riverfront, reestablishing pedestrian linkage. The richly articulated, high-performance glass and stainless steel facade maximizes daylighting while minimizing solar heat gain and

offers tenants a sophisticated, modern image in the Chicago Miesian tradition. The three-story lobby features a decorative screen of cherry wood and stainless steel, offset by marble floors.

Sustainable strategies include a green roof, use of river water for cooling, and incorporation of regional materials. During construction, river barges removed excavated material and delivered and removed equipment. Nearly all of the demolition and construction waste was recycled. The tower is extremely energy efficient: the innovative river-water cooling system eliminates cooling towers and chemicals, saving 5 million gallons (19 million liters) of treated water annually and greatly reducing energy use. Site placement maximizes the southern exposure for a public garden while minimizing solar gain on east and west facades. In addition to being an amenity for building tenants and the surrounding neighborhood, the public plaza was built to hide the river-water intake tanks.

Chicagoans have warmly welcomed 300 North LaSalle. The project redeveloped a prominently located, underused site that held a parking garage. It encourages pedestrian activity, provides a new riverfront plaza, and makes an elegant contribution to the Chicago skyline. The anchor tenant leases more than 600,000 square feet (56,000 m²) on 24 floors for its global headquarters, comprising about 1,400 employees. The development was completed in 2009 in a very difficult economy. Despite the stressful economic conditions, the project has been a

## PROJECT DATA

**Web Site**
www.300nlasalle.com

**Site Area**
1.2 ac (0.5 ha)

**Facilities**
1.3 million sf (120,774 m²) office
15,000 sf (1,394 m²)
retail/restaurant/entertainment
225 parking spaces

**Land Use**
office, retail, restaurant, parks/
open space

**Start/Completion Dates**
May 2006–March 2009

resounding success with a leased status of 96 percent. At 1.3 million square feet (121,000 m²), it is one of the largest office projects to be completed in Chicago in recent years. Hines sold the building in 2010, commanding the highest price per square foot ever paid for an office building in Chicago and making the sale one of the country's largest commercial real estate transactions that year.

## DEVELOPMENT TEAM

**Owner/Developer/Designer**
Cavenaugh + Cavenaugh LLC
Portland, Oregon
http://tenpod.org/tenants/
cavenaugh-cavenaugh-llc/

**Architect of Record**
Stack Architecture
Portland, Oregon
http://stackpdx.com/

## Jury STATEMENT

The LEED-Platinum Burnside Rocket features a ground-floor pub, two levels of creative office space, a top-floor restaurant, and outdoor terraces on each level. The four-story building is multifunctional: operable window panels double as canvases for local artists, the roof garden provides fresh produce for the restaurant, and water from an underground aquifer both cools the building and provides 17,000 liters of potable water each day.

# THE BURNSIDE ROCKET, Portland, Oregon

The Burnside Rocket is not your average project. The LEED-Platinum infill development in Portland features a ground-floor pub, two levels of shared office space, a top-floor restaurant, and a rooftop garden.

The four-story building is a case study in multifuctionality: operable window panels double as canvases for local artists, the roof garden provides fresh produce for the restaurant, and water from an underground aquifer both cools the building and yields 4,500 gallons (17,000 L) of potable water each day—profits from which the developer plans to donate to local public schools. The project embodies the do-it-yourself ethos of its host city and acts as a proper hinge along Burnside Street, the dividing line between north and south Portland.

The designer and owner of the Burnside Rocket, Kevin Cavenaugh, is not your average developer, either. He has made a name for himself in Portland designing and building small infill projects in burgeoning neighborhoods. "My goal is to change the world 3,000 square feet at a time, and the only way that will happen is if others take my ideas as support for their own practice," explains Cavenaugh. True to his words, all of his work—from CAD drawings to pro formas—is available on his website, a kind of open-source program for real estate developers.

This inclusive, cooperative milieu is evident throughout the Burnside Rocket. The commercial tenants are organized in a group called TENPOD, a creative service co-op of ten independently owned and operative businesses. These include architects, writers, engineers, designers, and craftspeople, all working in a shared 5,880-square-foot (539-m²) space where ideas and collaborative spirit flow freely. The ground-floor restaurant uses fresh produce from the rooftop garden, and each of the 24 moving art panels (four × six feet [1.2 × 1.8 m]) is painted by a different emerging artist who works in the neighborhood.

In a nod to East Burnside's unique architectural heritage, the Burnside Rocket features an arcade—a covered walkway that runs the length of the frontage—creating a protected pedestrian zone and outdoor dining area. Formerly a vacant property destined to become a parking lot, the narrow 38-foot (12-m) by 100-foot (30-m) site was considered by some to be unbuildable. Facing south and offering views of downtown Portland, the site did possess

redeeming qualities: it was adjacent to an indoor rock-climbing gym, frequent bus-service lines, and bike routes in the burgeoning arts and food scene of East Burnside. The four-story structure was built with off-the-shelf materials such as concrete masonry units and precast hollow-core concrete panels, keeping development costs down. The developer/designer used a bold color palette to enliven the facade, and the operable art panels provide light control for the building spaces and an iconic design.

The Burnside Rocket takes a whole-building approach to energy efficiency by integrating several green building measures, including ground-source heat pumps, operable windows, and a green roof. Designed to use just 50 percent of the energy of a typical commercial building, it is also the first office building built outside the downtown core without parking. An innovative geothermal system uses water from an on-site well to heat or cool air that is distributed through voids in the concrete floor slabs, and the rooftop garden captures and treats rainwater for 100 percent of the site area. Most important, many of the features that won LEED points also make the building a great place to work: roof gardens, operable windows, excellent air quality, and copious daylighting. The site was developed with funds from the Metro Regional Government's Transit Oriented Development Program. As part of the funding, an easement was secured to ensure that the developed space will remain mixed use for the next 30 years.

## PROJECT DATA

**Web Site**
www.burnsiderocket.com

**Site Area**
0.09 ac (0.04 ha)

**Facilities**
5,880 sf (546 m²) office
6,464 sf (601 m²) retail/restaurant/
entertainment

**Land Use**
retail, office, restaurant, open space

**Start/Completion Dates**
January 2006–June 2007

The bold design of the Burnside Rocket reflects the developer's willingness to take risks. These risks paid off, resulting in an iconic design and innovative systems, and a project that stands as an example for small-scale developers in a post–credit crunch world. As Cavenaugh explains, "the larger banks have become so fearful that ideas have taken a back seat. Successful projects like Burnside Rocket can help reverse the trend, providing new comparables and giving lenders confidence the next time an unconventional project comes across their desk."

PHOTOGRAPHY BY BRIAN FOULKES (ALL IMAGES)

## DEVELOPMENT TEAM

**Owner/Developer**
*Mosites Construction Company*
*Pittsburgh, Pennsylvania*
*www.mosites.com*

**Development Partners**
*East Liberty Development, Inc.*
*Pittsburgh, Pennsylvania*
*http://eastlibertypost.com*

*Urban Redevelopment*
*Authority of Pittsburgh*
*Pittsburgh, Pennsylvania*
*www.ura.org*

**Master Planner and Project Architect**
*The Design Alliance*
*Pittsburgh, Pennsylvania*
*www.tda-architects.com*

**Design Architect (Phase I)**
*Perfido Weiskopf Wagstaff + Goettel*
*Pittsburgh, Pennsylvania*
*www.pwwgarch.com*

**Design Architect (Phases III and IV)**
*Urban Design Associates*
*Pittsburgh, Pennsylvania*
*http://www.urbandesignassoci-ates.com/*

**Design Architect (Phase V)**
*RSP Architects*
*Minneapolis, Minnesota*
*http://www.rsparch.com/*

# EASTSIDE: PHASES I AND II,

**Pittsburgh, Pennsylvania** Located at the intersection of Center and South Highland avenues in Pittsburgh's East Liberty neighborhood, Eastside Phases I and II comprise a 5.1-acre (2.0-ha) mixed-use development that includes retail, restaurant, and office uses, with surface and deck parking. They include 4,724 square feet (439 m²) of office, 112,835 square feet (10,483 m²) of retail, and 472 parking spaces.

Eastside transforms a patchwork of 14.3 acres (5.8 ha) of distressed properties in the heart of Pittsburgh's east end. The project borrows economic strength from the more affluent adjacent neighborhoods of Shadyside, Friendship, and Highland Park to fuel the redevelopment of East Liberty, a commercial center plagued by decades of decline. Eastside I and II are complete, tenanted, and operating. Eastside V opened in July 2011 as a two-level Target store. Eastside III and IV are in planning.

The project is anchored by a Whole Foods Market, which opened in 2002 with sales that nearly tripled company projections, proving wrong those who thought the location was too urban and risky to support retail activity. Three more years of strategic marketing and continued sales growth at Whole Foods were still needed to ignite retailers' interest in Phase II, a mixed retail center. Phase II is anchored by Walgreens, Starbucks, the region's top-grossing Wine & Spirits store, and two of the city's top restaurants. Eastside I and II proved the site was viable, leading to a pledge by Target to build the first big-box store in the city. The emerging high-value tenant mix and market strength have fueled tenant interest in housing and Class A office for the final phase of the project.

In the 1950s, East Liberty was a thriving shopping district, with more than 500 businesses and a population of 14,000. By 1970, suburban flight and misguided urban renewal attempts had left the neighborhood a wasteland. The business district was plagued by the creation of an ill-advised pedestrian mall, which cut off access to the retail core, and by the implementation of a one-way ring road. In 1999, East Liberty Development, Inc. (ELDI), a community nonprofit, developed a plan to attract a broader range of shoppers, revive the urban street grid, and create jobs and housing. Believing in the neighborhood's potential, Mosites Construction

Eastside Phases I and II—the first phase of a five-phase classic "zipper" development—is designed to revitalize East Liberty, a community damaged by the urban renewal of the 1960s. The high-density, multilevel commercial scheme comprises 116,000 square feet of retail and office space, restaurants, and a grocery store.

## PROJECT DATA

**Web Site**
*www.shopeastside.net*

**Site Area**
*5.1 ac (2.0 ha)*

**Facilities**
*4,724 sf (439 m²) office space*
*112,835 sf (10,483 m²) retail/ restaurant/entertainment space*
*472 parking spaces*

**Land Use**
*retail, restaurant, office*

**Start/Completion Dates**
*June 2001–July 2006*

Company joined ELDI and the Urban Redevelopment Authority of Pittsburgh to redevelop the site. The eight parcels that form the site were acquired in stages, from 1999 through 2005. Development started in 2001. The first store opened in October 2002, and Phases I and II were completed in 2006.

The development has restored the urban street grid and reconnected East Liberty with its neighbors, both physically and economically. It draws shoppers from the immediate neighborhood as well as the wealthier surrounding communities. A new pedestrian bridge connects the Eastside development to Shadyside's Ellsworth and Highland shopping districts by spanning the Martin Luther King Jr. East Busway. The development achieved higher density by building a two-level structure, using grades and a deck, essentially creating two "ground levels."

The project is one of the first LEED (Leadership in Energy and Environmental Design)-Gold-certified projects in Pittsburgh and among the first LEED Core and Shell projects in the United States. Nearly all of the construction waste was recycled. Many of the building products were manufactured locally, and those made from recycled materials constituted over 30 percent of the building's materials. Highly reflective surfaces were used for the hardscape and roofs, thereby reducing the heat-island effect. The buildings use 17 percent less energy than typical retail buildings, the result of the high-performance curtain-wall system, enhanced insulation, and high-efficiency heating, ventilating, and air conditioning. Rainwater from the roof is piped to an underground cistern and used for on-site irrigation. Bike racks are provided on site for shoppers and employees, and showers are available for employees to encourage biking to work.

Eastside was the result of collaboration among public, community, and private partners, and it helped reset expectations for the neighborhood and its redevelopment. The project has demonstrated the viability of a commercial center that brings both the most disadvantaged and the wealthiest people in the region together by offering a mix of goods that appeal to all income levels. Eastside I and II have created 422 full-time-equivalent jobs, employing more than 150 neighborhood residents. ELDI holds regular job fairs and training programs to help neighborhood residents secure these jobs. Eastside has sparked economic growth and is drawing increasing numbers of tenants to East Liberty: for instance, Google has chosen the neighboring Bakery Square (a former Nabisco bakery) for its new Pittsburgh location.

Phases III and IV will be a transit-oriented development centered around East Liberty Station, the neighborhood's transit hub. Projected for completion in 2015, they will include nearly 100,000 square feet (9,300 m²) of office, 30,000 square feet (2,800 m²) of retail, 73 residential units, and 811 parking spaces.

PHOTOGRAPHY BY
ED MASSERY (34), ED MASSERY (36)
ALEXANDER DENMARSH (37)

## DEVELOPMENT TEAM

**Owner/Developer**
*Wilhelm Gienger Verwaltungs
GmbH
Munich, Germany
www.gienger.de*

**Design Architect**
*peterlorenzateliers
Innsbruck, Austria
www.peterlorenz.at*

## *Jury* STATEMENT

A 2,600-square-meter office
and retail development
opened in 2009 in Munich,
based on the idea of
an "energy spiral" that
creatively allows light
to filter throughout the
building, ENER[GIE]NGER
places great importance
on sustainability with a
250-square-meter solar
panel and a combined heat
and power plant for electric
and thermal energy.

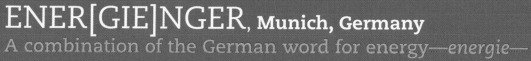

# ENER[GIE]NGER, Munich, Germany

A combination of the German word for energy—*energie*—and the name of the building material company—the Gienger Group—that occupies the space, ENER[GIE]NGER is innovative retail and exhibition space that uses the latest sustainable technologies.

The 2,600-square-meter (28,000-sf) space is a helix-shaped building clad entirely in solar and photovoltaic panels, glass, or metal elements. Serving as the showroom and outlet for Gienger products, the spiraling building structure forms a glittering point of attraction within an otherwise ordinary industrial park in Munich, Germany.

Gienger Group is a private, family-owned business that serves the state of Bavaria and forms part of a bigger group of companies serving all parts of Germany under a common holding company. The building material company sells bathroom equipment, heating and cooling systems, and all other equipment that tradesmen need to appropriately fit out residential and commercial buildings.

The site once housed the original Gienger building, built in 1968 as a showroom, wholesale store, and warehouse for steel pipes. In 2009, the warehouse was moved to a different location, the former buildings demolished, and an architectural competition held under the theme "energy and the Gienger Group business." The winning design, constrained to the existing site of 6,000 square meters (64,600 sf), was expected to combine a showroom with a retail component, sufficient parking lots, and landscaping aiming to become a flagship building for the Gienger Group.

The winning architect, the Innsbruck-based Peter Lorenz, used the concept of an "energy spiral." The architectural form creates a tunnel effect, with the spiral motif carried from the glass-walled lobby, which includes the showroom, through to the back entrance. Each spiral band is slightly offset, allowing narrow windows to illuminate and throw slanting rays of light through the elongated space. The roof as well as the south exposure is made up of photovoltaic panels, and the remainder of the building is clad in dark-blue metal and glass panels, giving the building a futuristic appearance.

The inside of the building—the ceiling, walls, staircases, and handrails—is practical and simple, detailed with a very technical look, so as not to detract from the product displays. The 1,500-square-meter (16,000-sf) exhibition hall fills the full height of the building at the entrance, and then the building is separated into three different levels as one moves through the facility. To optimize the space in a more efficient way, the site hosts the retail exhibition in the upper levels and the 800-square-meter (8,600-sf) wholesale store extends to the middle of the building on the ground floor.

On the top level of the exhibition hall is an "educational energy trail," featuring a variety of energy-efficient technologies and heating and cooling systems using alternative energies. A low-energy-house exhibit displays a combination of these systems. The exhibition hall is wide and open, with extensive daylighting through the glass-wall entrance that overlooks the outer entrance and landscaped areas. The innovative design at ENER[GIE]NGER—both in building design and the products on exhibit—raises the bar for nonstorefront retail uses.

## PROJECT DATA

**Web Site**
*www.peterlorenz.at*

**Site Area**
*0.6 hectare (1.5 ac)*

**Facilities**
*2,600 m² (27,986 sf) office and exhibition space*

**Land Use**
*retail, office, industrial/warehouse*

**Start/Completion Dates**
*2008–November 2009*

## DEVELOPMENT TEAM

**Developer**
Galotti S.p.A
Milan, Italy
www.galotti.it

**Owner**
Quorum S.G.R.p.A.
Milan, Italy
www.quorumsgr.it

**Design Architect**
FGS Goring & Straja Architects
Milan, Italy
www.gasarchitects.com

# *Jury* STATEMENT

A 16,000-square-meter office development built in the Expo 2015 district of Milan on a previously undeveloped site, Perseo is designed to stand at the intersection of environmental sustainability, urban integration, and internal flexibility.

# PERSEO, **Milan, Italy**  Located on the outskirts of Milan, Perseo is a 16,000-square-meter (177,200-sf) office development built to the highest level of sustainable design. Comprising two buildings connected by a slender four-story bridge, the project is capped by an expansive brise-soleil that shades the glass facade and uses passive design to reduce energy use by more than half of what the code requires.

Completed in January 2011, Perseo is located near the grounds of World Expo 2015 and is designed to anticipate the future needs of Milan through energy-efficient and intelligent design.

Milan enjoys low unemployment and a per capita income that is almost twice the national average. With the World Expo—and its theme of sustainable development—slated to arrive in the suburban area of Pero, the vacant site where Perseo now stands became a desirable location for office development. Although outside the central business district, the project is near a major hub of Milan's freeway system and two subway stations.

The property was originally slated for a run-of-the-mill office building until the developer, Milan-based Galotti, stepped in. Dedicated to balancing its projects with the surrounding environment, for 60 years Galotti has developed shopping malls, retail parks, and office buildings throughout Italy. The developer retained the services of Goring & Straja Architects in 2006 with the purpose of delivering a next-generation office building at the unlikely suburban location.

Perseo was designed to stand at the intersection of environmental sustainability, urban integration, and internal flexibility. The developer refers to it as a "triple-A" development—a Class A office space, grade A certified for sustainability, and built to be a high-quality and flexible work environment. The building is oriented toward the southwest to maximize solar

gain in the winter. To protect it from solar gain in the summer months, a massive horizontal brise-soleil shades the facade, and operable windows promote passive cooling throughout the building. The bridge that connects the two structures also functions as a chimney, allowing accumulated heat to escape through the roof during summer nights. A 250-square-meter (2,690-sf) photovoltaic array buttresses the project's energy load, and an advanced cooling system reduces energy use.

Currently home to a single tenant, Il Sole 24 Ore, the office development was designed to adapt to the demands of future users: the depth of the buildings is 18–19 meters (59–62 feet) with minimal internal structural columns, enabling users to create large offices and meeting rooms or to leave an open-plan workspace. The twin-building design creates the potential for two separate lobbies while also framing courtyard space. The passive design and advanced building systems reduce operating costs, making the building a desirable location for many potential tenants.

## PROJECT DATA

**Web Site**
*www.galotti.it/perseo/*

**Site Area**
*0.67 hectare (1.7 ac)*

**Facilities**
*15,961 m² (171,800 sf) office space*

**Land Use**
*office, open space, surface parking*

**Start/Completion Dates**
*January 2008–January 2011*

PHOTOGRAPHY BY
ENRICO CANO (ALL IMAGES)

Perseo stands as a new benchmark for future developments on the urban fringe. Its significant energy savings and innovative passive design greatly reduce carbon dioxide emissions and operating costs, making it an attractive option for future tenants.

# Mixed Use | WINNERS

## DEVELOPMENT TEAM

**Owner/Developer**
*LandCorp*
*Perth, Western Australia,*
*Australia*
*www.landcorp.com.au*

**Master Planner**
*Taylor Burrell Barnett*
*Subiaco, Western Australia,*
*Australia*
*http://tbbplanning.com.au*

**Design Architects**
*Woods Bagot*
*Adelaide, South Australia,*
*Australia*
*www.woodsbagot.com*

*Jones Coulter Young*
*Perth, Western Australia,*
*Australia*
*www.jcy.net*

## Jury STATEMENT

The 62-acre Mandurah Ocean Marina is an integrated development, mixing maritime, residential, commercial, and recreational uses. Built on a strip of underused state-owned land in Mandurah, Australia, the marina fulfills a 30-year community vision and has become an economic boon for the area.

# MANDURAH OCEAN MARINA,

**Mandurah, Australia** The 62-hectare (153-ac) Mandurah Ocean Marina is a waterfront hub and major tourist destination adjacent to the central business district of Mandurah, a city located about an hour's drive south of Perth, Western Australia's capital. With a thriving tourism industry, Mandurah is one of the fastest-growing urban areas in Australia.

Fulfilling a 30-year community vision for a world-class boating and tourism facility, Mandurah Ocean Marina overcame major stakeholder differences, enabling positive outcomes for all involved: adjoining landowners, clubs, and residents. The development was created on a strip of underused—and in some areas derelict—oceanfront land. Composed of North Harbour and South Harbour, linked by a pedestrian bridge, the development offers a mix of residences, hotels, shops, restaurants and cafés, entertainment venues, mooring facilities for large and small boats, and activities for boating and fishing enthusiasts. Specifically, it includes 2,500 square meters (26,900 sf) of office space; 16,000 square meters (172,200 sf) of retail, restaurant, and entertainment facilities; a 24,000-square-meter (258,300-sf) marina; 281 hotel rooms; 410 residences; and 1,700 parking spaces.

The project includes two hotels: the Seashells Resort, offering 66 luxury one- and two-bedroom suites and beach villas, and the Mirvac Sebel Hotel, with 89 guest rooms and suites. Both hotels include conference facilities. Dolphin Quay offers restaurants, cafés, specialty shops, and market stalls in a wharf-style setting. The Mandurah Performing Arts Centre includes several theaters and other performance spaces with seating for up to 800 patrons.

Mandurah Ocean Marina creates an urban experience for pedestrians with its main streets, promenades, and boardwalks. The marina seamlessly links to Mandurah's traditional city center. The core objective of community accessibility was achieved with 90 percent of the marina being accessible to the general public, and with 40 percent of the public open space comprising foreshore areas, boardwalks, and landscaped streets and plazas. Venetian-style canals in South Harbour lend an unusual flavor to the development.

The A$80 million project began in 1999 when the site was acquired by the developer, LandCorp. Construction began that same year. The development opened to the public in 2001 and will be completed by the end of 2011.

Mandurah Ocean Marina has been an economic success for the developer and the local community. In addition to more than 100 jobs created during the infrastructure construction phase, about 600 jobs resulted from building construction. The project will create more than 600 full-time jobs and generate about A$900 million in economic activity over the next 20 years, according to estimates. Land sales have broken all records for the area. Building sites ranging from 217 square meters (2,336 sf) to 1,010 square meters (10,872 sf) have sold at prices from A$265,000 for a site on the mainland to A$6.26 million for a 3,000-square-meter (32,000-sf) waterfront site. Some 162 development sites have been sold since the first land release in 2001. Mandurah Ocean Marina has become a national tourism destination and is Australia's most-awarded marina development, with more than 15 awards.

## PROJECT DATA

**Web Site**
www.mandurahocean
marina.com.au

**Site Area**
60 ha (148 ac)

**Facilities**
2,500 m² (26,900 sf) office (4,000 m²/43,000 sf at buildout)
16,000 m² (177,200 sf) retail, restaurant, and entertainment (21,000 m²/226,040 sf at buildout)
24,000 m² (258,300 sf) industrial
10 single-family units (20 at buildout)
400 multifamily units (600 at buildout)
281 hotel rooms (350 at buildout)
1,700 parking spaces

**Land Use**
residential, retail, office, marina, restaurant, entertainment, parks/open space

**Start/Completion Dates**
1999–2011

PHOTOGRAPHY BY RICHARD GALE,
GALE FORCE PHOTOGRAPHY (ALL IMAGES)

## DEVELOPMENT TEAM

**Owner/Developer**
*East West Partners*
*Avon, Colorado*
*www.ewpartners.com*

**Master Planner**
*Design Workshop, Inc.*
*Denver, Colorado*
*www.designworkshop.com*

**Design Architect
(Commons Park)**
*Civitas, Inc.*
*Denver, Colorado*
*www.civitasinc.com*

## Jury STATEMENT

Integrated into the downtown grid of Denver and built on the site of a former rail yard, Riverfront Park is a new urban neighborhood with more than 1,400 residential units and 62,000 square feet of retail space. Designed and built under a form-based zoning code, Riverfront Park also features four parks and a landmark bridge, reclaiming the riverfront from an abandoned brownfield.

# RIVERFRONT PARK, Denver, Colorado

Part of the larger redevelopment of the Central Platte Valley, Riverfront Park is a 23-acre (9.2-ha) master-planned community that extends the urban core of downtown Denver.

Built on the site of a former rail yard, the residential neighborhood contains 1,430 residential units—a mix of for-sale, rental, and affordable residences—with a planned capacity of 2,142 residential units upon completion and 62,000 square feet (5,760 m²) of retail at the heart of the community. A single-mast suspension bridge 200 feet (61 m) tall connects Riverfront Park to Denver's Lower Downtown (LoDo) district. Commons Park, intended to be downtown Denver's equivalent of New York City's Central Park, is the focal point and main public amenity for the master-planned community.

The Central Platte Valley, a broad swath between a major interstate and Denver's downtown core, was once nearly 500 acres (200 ha) of discarded land and abandoned rail yards. One of the major gateways to Denver's downtown, this derelict industrial area has been the focus of public/private redevelopment efforts for the past two decades, beginning with the creation of the Central Platte Valley Comprehensive Plan in 1986. The plan focused on consolidating the active rail lines, zoning land for mixed-use development, creating a major regional open-space amenity, and spurring market-rate housing development; at the time, very little housing existed in the downtown core. In 1991, the surplus land, owned by six different railroads, was sold to Trillium Development, opening up more than 6 million square feet (557,000 m²) of land for development in the valley.

In 1999, East West Partners purchased 23 acres (9.2 ha) from Trillium along the east side of Commons Park—approximately 12 city blocks. To demonstrate its long-term commitment to the area, the developer split the cost of the Millennium Bridge with the city and took over the construction process, ensuring the delivery of an iconic landmark and a direct pedestrian link between the LoDo neighborhood and Riverfront Park's piazza-like central town square and Commons Park. The master plan, by Design Workshop, complements Denver's central business district: the plan fosters an urban, residential character distinct from downtown but consistent enough in form and density to ensure a smooth transition from the surrounding areas to Riverfront Park.

No residence in the neighborhood is more than a block from Commons Park, in the center of the development, or from the Cherry Creek Greenway, a privately funded 40-mile (64-km) network of trails. Pedestrian bridges enable bikers, walkers, and joggers to cross the river and rail lines to adjacent neighborhoods. The 130-foot (40-m) span of Millennium Bridge, the most iconic of these, is widely recognized by its 200-foot (61-m) mast and cables. Denver Skatepark, at the northern edge of the development, is the largest free public skateboard park in the nation.

Buildings at Riverfront Park are modern in design but with a nod to traditional Denver forms and materials. Most of the buildings are flat-roofed red or tan brick. Some make use of granite, sandstone, glass curtain walls, and pastel stucco. Metal overhangs and balconies add interest. Building types range from three-story townhouses to 23-story high rises; many feature retail space at the ground level. Parking is in structures or underground.

Besides the physical changes Riverfront Park brought to the city, it has served the community by establishing the Riverfront Park Community Foundation, a nonprofit with the goal of incubating arts and education programs throughout the city and funding projects that improve the lives of downtown residents and workers. The foundation is supported solely by residents of Riverfront Park through a 0.5 percent transfer assessment on every home sale. The foundation generates about $300,000 annually. Projects funded thus far include preservation of wetlands, construction of a dog park, and public art installations. Grants have also been used for after-school programs, community health initiatives, art exhibits, and cultural programming.

## PROJECT DATA

**Web Site**
*www.riverfrontpark.com*

**Site Area**
*23 ac (9.2 ha)*

**Facilities**
*62,000 sf (5,760 m²) retail*
*26,000 sf (2,415 m²) civic*
*7,000 sf (650 m²) education*
*1,430 multifamily units (2,142 at buildout)*

**Land Uses**
*residential, retail, restaurant, entertainment, civic, park/ open space, parking*

**Start/Completion Dates**
*June 2000–2013 (projected)*

PHOTOGRAPHY COURTESY OF
EAST WEST PARTNERS (ALL IMAGES)

Riverfront Park demonstrates the power of public/private collaboration for the redevelopment of a large urban neighborhood. The project reclaimed the city's waterfront from an abandoned rail yard, brought new life to the city's core, and connected it to neighboring districts. Per square foot sales prices for the residences are 50 percent higher than those in adjacent neighborhoods. Rental rates and occupancy percentages are in the top 5 percent for the metro area. The neighborhood's proximity to a multimodal transit facility—light rail and local and regional bus service—allowed East West Partners to reduce the parking spaces at Riverfront Park, creating a true urban district.

# *Residential* | WINNERS

## DEVELOPMENT TEAM

**Owner/Developer**
*New Hope Housing, Inc.*
*Houston, Texas*
*www.newhopehousing.com*

**Architect**
*Glassman Shoemake Maldonado*
*Architects*
*Houston, Texas*
*http://gsmarchitects.net/*

## Jury STATEMENT

Brays Crossing is the conversion of the former HouTex Inn—a 1960s-style derelict motel located along a major freeway—into 149 single-room-occupancy apartments for low-income citizens. Operated without the use of government rent subsidies, the project integrates a public art display into the building design, turning a former eyesore into a community canvas.

# BRAYS CROSSING, Houston, Texas

Brays Crossing shatters the stereotype of low-income, single-room-occupancy (SRO) housing, proving that it can be both visually attractive and affordable and built debt-free and without government subsidy.

Developed by New Hope Housing, a Houston-based nonprofit, the community features 149 SRO units along with community space and on-site social services, in seven brightly colored buildings that were formerly a dilapidated and blighted motel. The project is clad with a colorful steel mural that attenuates sound from the nearby highway, a functional solution that extends the rich mural tradition of Houston's East End neighborhood.

Brays Crossing is the fifth project in Houston developed by New Hope Housing, an independent nonprofit founded in 1993 that is dedicated to providing stabilized housing for single adults living on limited incomes. New Hope Housing developed Houston's first SRO, the Hamilton Street Residences, in 1995 and has provided more than 4,000 individuals—many of whom ultimately transition to traditional housing—with high-quality, supportive housing, helping alleviate homelessness in Houston.

In 2006, the city of Houston approached New Hope to redevelop the former HouTex Inn. Located in Houston's Hispanic East End, where the area median income is $13,000 annually, the motel complex was built in 1963 to house NASA contractors; however, over the years it had become a derelict, crime-ridden, certified public nuisance. New Hope worked with the city, neighborhood leaders, housing tax credit investors, and private foundations and businesses to redevelop the property.

The partners could not have picked a more challenging site: a slender parcel hemmed in by a busy highway on one side and a cemetery on the other. Making matters more difficult was the state of the existing property, which had fallen into complete disrepair. The developer brought all seven buildings up to code, converting the motel rooms into 149 SRO apartments for low-income citizens. The nonprofit worked with local authorities to install sidewalks and a lighted path under the Brays Bayou Bridge, giving residents of the formerly isolated site

access to shopping and recreation. Designed for a livable and sustainable future, the project is within a one-mile (1.6-km) radius of a full-service grocery store, a convenience store, several restaurants, and two METRO bus lines.

Each of the units at Brays Crossing includes a microwave, refrigerator, and private bath. A centrally located building includes shared spaces: community rooms with televisions and a library, a community kitchen, a fully equipped business center, laundry rooms, and a social service coordinator office. Three intimate courtyard spaces within the property encourage a sense of community among the residents. One of the larger courtyards includes a fountain; another includes an outdoor cooking area and lawn.

Brays Crossing features a large public art display that is integral to the design and function of the project. Glassman Shoemake Maldonado Architects devised an inventive way to attenuate noise generated by the adjacent highway through four steel murals—each towering 14 feet (4 m) high and 48 feet (15 m) long. The facade serves as a colossal canvas for Chicana artist Carmen Lomas Garza, who designed the whimsical murals using the motif of *papel picada,* or Mexican cut-paper folk art. The contiguous art installation faces the busy highway, turning a former eyesore into a community canvas and neighborhood landmark.

New Hope Housing uses a debt-free business model for its SRO projects, able to operate the developments without the use of government rent subsidies. Rental rates, which are

## PROJECT DATA

**Web Site**
*www.newhopehousing.com/brayscrossing*

**Site Area**
*1.97 ac (0.8 ha)*

**Facilities**
*149 multifamily units*
*56 parking spaces*

**Land Use**
*residential, open space*

**Start/Completion Dates**
*January 2009–March 2010*

PHOTOGRAPHY BY
BRUCE GLASS PHOTOGRAPHY

approximately $415 a month for adults living only on limited incomes (approximately $1,200 a month), cover operations, maintenance, and utility costs. Brays Crossing was leased up and stabilized in less than nine months. "Brays Crossing proves that affordable, supportive housing can be high quality and a vibrant asset that both stabilizes lives and improves neighborhoods," said Joy Horak-Brown, executive director of New Hope Housing.

## DEVELOPMENT TEAM

**Developer**
*The Bozzuto Group*
*Greenbelt, Maryland*
*www.bozzuto.com*

**Owners**
*The Bozzuto Group*
*Greenbelt, Maryland*
*www.bozzuto.com*

*Gould Property Co.*
*Winter Park, Florida*
*www.gouldandcompany.net*

*J.P. Morgan*
*New York, New York*
*www.jpmorgan.com*

**Architect**
*Design Collective, Inc.*
*Baltimore, Maryland*
*www.designcollective.com*

## Jury STATEMENT

On the site of a former coal yard, the Fitzgerald comprises 275 apartments and 25,000 square feet of retail in midtown Baltimore. Adjacent to the light-rail line and within walking distance of Penn Station, the new residential building is a leading investment in a larger neighborhood redevelopment effort led by the University of Baltimore.

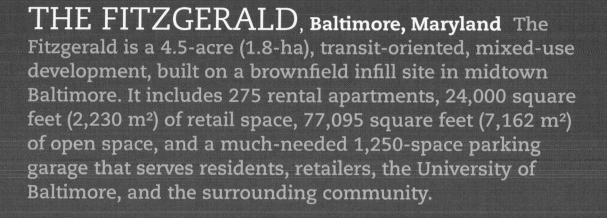

# THE FITZGERALD, Baltimore, Maryland

The Fitzgerald is a 4.5-acre (1.8-ha), transit-oriented, mixed-use development, built on a brownfield infill site in midtown Baltimore. It includes 275 rental apartments, 24,000 square feet (2,230 m²) of retail space, 77,095 square feet (7,162 m²) of open space, and a much-needed 1,250-space parking garage that serves residents, retailers, the University of Baltimore, and the surrounding community.

It is the largest residential property in the city to secure LEED (Leadership in Energy and Environmental Design) certification; it includes a vegetated green roof, electric car charging stations, and numerous in-unit green features.

Named for writer F. Scott Fitzgerald, who once lived two blocks from the site, the Fitzgerald was built on a site that was a university-owned surface parking lot and before that a Goodyear Tire facility and a railroad coal yard. These uses conferred a brownfield status to the site, which required remediation. The development team obtained approval for a Response Action Plan from the state of Maryland to allow remediation of the site for residential purposes.

The Fitzgerald is the cornerstone of an extensive redevelopment effort led by the University of Baltimore to revitalize the city's Midtown neighborhood and make the district more pedestrian oriented. The Fitzgerald, which represents a $75 million investment, abuts the sidewalk with a transparent glass facade, providing interest for passersby and "eyes on the street" for enhanced security. The mix of uses helps enliven the district at all times of the day.

Built at a density of 60 units per acre, the transit-oriented development is located adjacent to a light-rail station and two blocks from Penn Station, the city's main train station, which is served by regional and long-distance rail lines. The Fitzgerald is within walking distance of the University of Baltimore and the Maryland Institute College of Art, the opera and symphony, dining, shopping, and services. It rates a Walk Score® of 86, indicating a very walkable environment.

To achieve LEED certification, the building was designed to run with 70 percent of its electricity from renewable sources. Nearby transit and walkability allow residents to reduce use of personal vehicles. Water consumption is reduced through the use of dual-flush toilets and low-flow plumbing fixtures. The garage offers bike racks and preferred parking for hybrid vehicles and car sharing. The garage is the first public garage in Maryland to have on-site electric car charging stations. More than 90 percent of the project's construction waste was recycled, and more than 25 percent of the materials used to build the project were sourced within 500 miles (805 km).

Apartments include studios and one- and two-bedroom units. Amenities include a fitness center, a business center and conference facilities, a movie theater, an outdoor swimming pool, and concierge service. Units feature Energy Star appliances, low-flow showerheads and faucets, dual-flush toilets, low-E windows, and paint and carpet with low volatile organic compound emissions.

The building, designed by the Design Collective, wraps around two courtyards and consists of five levels: a ground floor of retail and four stories of apartment units. One courtyard includes a swimming pool. A glass-enclosed walkway connects two sections of the building at every level. The clean, contemporary design uses a metal-clad exterior and large areas of glass with bay windows and metal balconies to add interest. Interiors, designed by RD Jones, are casual and contemporary, with stone, wood, and tile finishes.

## PROJECT DATA

**Web Site**
www.fitzgeraldbaltimore.com

**Site Area**
4.5 ac (1.8 ha)

**Facilities**
275 multifamily units
24,000 sf (2,230 m²) retail/
restaurant/entertainment
1,250 parking spaces

**Land Use**
residential, retail, open space,
parking garage

**Start/Completion Dates**
October 2008–October 2010

The Fitzgerald is a joint venture between the Bozzuto Group and private investors, with the University of Baltimore retaining ownership of the land. The developers negotiated a ground lease for the land, which generates an income stream for the university. From the city's point of view, this project turned a non-income-producing publicly owned parking lot into a revenue-producing development that still provides parking for the university. The old surface lot contained 580 parking spaces, whereas the new garage offers 950 designated parking spaces for students and university employees. The parking garage was the first phase to open, providing early cash flow for the developer as the remaining components were completed.

The Fitzgerald has been highly successful financially. Financing for the project was received during the height of the nation's economic downturn, a time when few developments were able to secure financing. It was the fastest-leasing apartment development in the city of Baltimore, with an average of 29 units per month absorption—despite opening during one of the worst recessions in the nation's history. The 24,000-square-foot (2,230-m²) retail space is entirely leased: Barnes & Noble occupies 20,000 square feet (1,858 m²), and the remainder is leased to two restaurants.

PHOTOGRAPHY BY THE BOZZUTO GROUP

## DEVELOPMENT TEAM

**Developer**
Gateway Foundation
St. Louis, Missouri
www.gateway-foundation.org

**Owner**
City of St. Louis
St. Louis, Missouri

**Landscape Architect**
Nelson Byrd Woltz Landscape
Architects
Charlottesville, Virginia
www.nbwla.com

## *Jury* STATEMENT

With a design that draws
on St. Louis's chief natural
feature—its rivers—the
2.9-acre Citygarden
has attracted diverse
users, catalyzed nearby
development, and changed
perceptions of downtown.
Situated on two blocks of
the underused Gateway
Mall, the active sculpture
garden has drawn visitors,
residents, and workers back
to the heart of St. Louis.

# CITYGARDEN, **St. Louis, Missouri** Citygarden, which opened in July 2009 on two of the Gateway Mall's key blocks, was aimed at creating an active and enticing space that would attract a diverse public, alter perceptions of downtown, and catalyze downtown development.

The 2.9-acre (1.2-ha) rectilinear open space comprises a sculpture garden with interactive art, imaginative and whimsical water features, and dining and picnicking venues. The inviting park has spurred redesign of the Gateway Mall, elevated the status of public art in St. Louis, and been a boon to local businesses. Simply put by St. Louis mayor Francis Slay, "Citygarden is the most significant development to take place in St. Louis since the completion of the Gateway Arch nearly 50 years ago."

For nearly a century, St. Louis's Gateway Mall, a 1.1-mile (1.8-km) ribbon of grass and trees that unfurls west from the Gateway Arch, has held the potential to be a grand civic space. That potential had been left unfulfilled: the mall has long been devoid of interest and people and has been a hindrance to downtown development. Despite the long odds, the Gateway Foundation, a nonprofit dedicated to supporting efforts to acquire, create, or improve art and urban design, managed to transcend the issues that had bedeviled the site over the years. The foundation contributed $25 million, not including the cost of the sculptures, to build the city-owned park.

Citygarden was tailored to the St. Louis area: its landscaping draws on the area's chief natural feature—its rivers—as well as on the site's cultural history. Its limestone arc wall 550 feet (179 m) long evokes the Mississippi's and Missouri's limestone bluffs; the serpentine seat wall 1,100 feet (335 m) long mirrors the course of the river itself. The hill on its northwest corner references the Native American burial mounds that once dotted the local landscape, and pathways follow old city alleyways and property lines. The garden—with native trees and grasses—is entirely distinctive to the region it inhabits.

The urban open space has also had a positive effect on the surrounding real estate market and businesses. Although the St. Louis market remains sluggish, local brokers and management companies indicate that the park is considered a strong amenity

and a contributing factor to high occupancy rates. Local shops and ground-floor retail establishments have benefited from the increased foot traffic, a sign that Citygarden is producing more than "island visits"—economic development parlance for users who visit a venue and then return home—and thus contributing to the vitality of downtown.

The urban park, designed by Charlottesville, Virginia–based Nelson Byrd Woltz Landscape Architects, was planned with social equity in mind. It is open every day, without walls or fences surrounding it or any prescribed points of entrance or exit. Through the use of ramps, paving coloration, and textured stone, the park is accessible to the able bodied and those with disabilities alike. "It has given St. Louis the kind of place—now uncommon—where people of all backgrounds can interact; it is a 'social condenser,'" proclaimed the *New Republic*.

Citygarden is part city park, part sculpture garden, standing as an example of the increasing role public art plays in the revitalization and rebranding of cities. Interactive sculptures—24 in all—are scattered throughout the site, including works by Fernand Léger, Aristide Maillol, Jim Dine, and Bernar Venet. It also includes a state-of-the-art LED video wall that displays art and films, a pool with a six-foot (two-m) waterfall, and a glass pavilion café. The varied topography, walkways, and walls separate the park into various "rooms," each with its own distinct feel and purpose.

## PROJECT DATA

**Web Site**
*www.citygardenstl.org*

**Site Area**
*2.9 ac (1.2 ha)*

**Land Uses**
*open space, restaurant*

**Start/Completion Dates**
*January 2007–July 2009*

The success of Citygarden has led to an effort to develop the rest of the Gateway Mall. A national design competition was held to redesign the grounds of the Gateway Arch and the St. Louis riverfront, linking them better with downtown and across the river, an initiative known as CityArchRiver 2015. Walter Metcalfe, board member of the CityArchRiver 2015 Foundation, believes that the success of Citygarden has made the larger redevelopment effort possible. "The political leadership and the community at large became believers in design-led development to address all the impacts great public spaces can have—civic, social, aesthetic, environmental, and economic."

PHOTOGRAPHY BY STEVE HALL (68)
HEDRICH BLESSING; STEVE HALL (70), HEDRICH
BLESSING; STEVE HALL (70), HEDRICH BLESSING;
DEBBIE FRANKE (71)

boosters for the transit investment itself, and fostering development along the corridor by encouraging others to follow their lead. Cleveland State University has completed about $50 million in projects along the avenue and plans on investing another $150 million in new development. The university has also reconfigured its master plan to recognize the Euclid Avenue BRT and new development as a campus amenity.

Noninstitutional development projects along the corridor often take the form of reuse or renovation of historic structures. The Baker Electric Building was built in 1910 as an automobile showroom and is listed on the National Register of Historic Places. It now houses offices and labs for local startup companies in 52,000 square feet (5,000 m²) of space that will soon be LEED (Leadership in Energy and Environmental Design) certified. Like many Euclid Avenue projects, it qualified for brownfield redevelopment grants and was also financed in part with new markets tax credits. Other renovation and revitalization projects include East 4th Street within the Gateway District. Formerly a disused alleyway, it has been transformed through adaptive use into a thriving pedestrian-oriented restaurant and residential center.

The Euclid Avenue Transportation Project was the first BRT project in the country to receive funding from the Federal Transit Administration's New Starts Program. It was considered a pilot project to gauge the ability of BRT to attract new development in the same way that rail transit has been proven to do. Cleveland's Euclid Avenue BRT, also known as the HealthLine because it connects two major medical facilities and their associated development, was carefully designed to have the look and feel of light rail. Tickets are purchased in stations

## PROJECT DATA

**Web Site**
www.rtahealthline.com/project-overview.asp

**Site Area**
6.8 mi (10.9 km)

**Facilities**
3.1 million sf (288,000 m²) office
2.5 million sf (232,260 m²) retail/restaurant/entertainment
1 million sf (92,900 m²) education
4,460 multifamily units
176 hotel rooms
6,787 parking spaces

**Land Use**
office, residential, retail, education, restaurant, entertainment, hotel

**Start/Completion Dates**
2002–Ongoing

PHOTOGRAPHY BY
CRAIG KUHNER (ALL IMAGES)

rather than on the bus, and passenger boarding for most of the route takes place in the median rather than curbside, avoiding conflicts with cars, pedestrians, and bicyclists. This attention to detail has paid off: two-thirds of all building permits in Cleveland are issued for sites within a half mile (0.8 km) of the Euclid Avenue corridor, and ridership is up 54 percent over traditional bus ridership along the same route.

Although some projects have been delayed by the recent nationwide downturn, overall the corridor has bucked national trends and as the economy comes back is now poised to again become one of the United States' great urban boulevards. Cities around the country are now looking to Cleveland as a model for successful BRT thanks to the thoughtful and comprehensive public investment that has leveraged itself many times over in private sector and institutional dollars.

## DEVELOPMENT TEAM

**Developer/Owner**
*PUB, the National Water Agency*
*Singapore*
*www.pub.gov.sg*

**Engineering Consultant**
*Camp Dresser & McKee*
*International*
*Cambridge, Massachusetts*
*www.cdm.com*

**Design Architect**
*Architects Team 3 Pte Ltd*
*Singapore*
*www.at3s.com.sg*

## *Jury* STATEMENT

Marina Barrage is a dam that creates a freshwater lake in the heart of Singapore, forming a reservoir for drinking water, a tidal barrier to prevent flooding in low-lying areas, and a water-recreation venue. The development— part municipal project, part educational facility— exemplifies Singapore's approach to sustainable water management, collecting rainwater runoff from approximately one-sixth of the city-state's area

# MARINA BARRAGE, Singapore

Bridging the mouth of the Marina Channel, Marina Barrage creates Singapore's 15th freshwater reservoir and its first in the heart of the city. Designed and developed by the Public Utilities Board (PUB), Singapore's national water agency, the barrage and reservoir stand as an international model for urbanized areas.

Part infrastructure project, part new urban park, Marina Barrage features an 11,000-square-meter (118,400-sf) green roof, a jetty for boats to dock, a water-sports center for sailing and rowing, an exhibition gallery for public education, and commercial space for restaurants and retail use.

Marina Barrage fulfills a 20-year vision of former prime minister Lee Kuan Yew to create a public reservoir in the center of Singapore and help address the city-state's water resource challenges. Prior to independence in 1965, Singapore had been entirely dependent on Malaysia for a supply of freshwater. Since then, however, the city-state has set upon a path to water self-sufficiency, cleaning its rivers, building reservoirs, and establishing the technological capacity to reclaim freshwater. Marina Barrage, capable of providing 10 percent of the nation's freshwater supply, represents the culmination of these efforts.

The reservoir attracts year-round water recreation, contributing to an entirely new wave of downtown lifestyle options. The constant water level is attractive to enthusiasts of boating, canoeing, and dragon-boat racing as well as to water taxis, which can serve the new residential and commercial venues. The large green roof provides an open, landscaped space that can be used for picnics, concerts, and movie screenings. The waterfront land, now unaffected by the tide and associated mud flats, is more attractive for development purposes.

Marina Barrage is a multipurpose civic project: the freshwater reservoir boosts Singapore's water supply, collects and treats rainwater runoff, and prevents flooding. The catchment area of the reservoir is approximately 10,000 hectares (25,000 ac)—the largest in the city—draining rainwater from one-sixth the area of Singapore. As a tidal barrier, the Marina Barrage's 350-meter (383-yd) length will keep seawater out during periods of high tide and alleviate

flooding in low-lying areas of the city, such as Chinatown, Jalan Besar, and Geylang. When heavy rains occur during low tide, the barrage's crest gates—each 30 meters (33 yd) wide, five meters (five yd) high, and weighing 70 tons—remain closed, and giant drainage pumps pump excess water out to sea.

More than an engineering showpiece, Marina Barrage is designed, constructed, and operated on green principles, exemplifying Singapore's commitment to sustainable water management. PUB is tasked with managing the highly urbanized city-state's water supply, water catchment, and wastewater in an integrated manner. At Marina Barrage, the public utility educates the community on important environmental and water issues through the Sustainable Singapore Gallery and creates a new outdoor recreational venue for citizens. The green roof insulates the building and pump rooms, reducing the building's air-conditioning load. The project also deploys an array of 405 solar panels, which supplements the daytime power requirements of the barrage.

Since opening in 2008, Marina Barrage has welcomed more than 2 million visitors and received numerous awards for excellence in engineering and sustainability, standing as a water conservation model for urbanized, seafront cities across the globe. Singapore's circumstances necessitated a bold and innovative solution to provide a new supply of drinking water, increased flood control, and recreational opportunities for its citizens. "The three benefits [Marina Barrage] brings will transform the waterscape of Singapore and be something all Singaporeans can enjoy and be a part of," said PUB's chief executive Khoo Teng Chye.

## PROJECT DATA

**Web Site**
*www.pub.gov.sg/marina*

**Site Area**
*4.9 ha (12 ac)*

**Facilities**
*9,079 m² (97,725 sf) industrial space*
*9,625 m² (103,602 sf) open space*
*3,027 m² (32,582 sf) retail/ restaurant/entertainment*
*890 m² (9,579 sf) education*
*98 parking spaces*

**Land Use**
*industrial, open space, retail, restaurant, education*

**Start/Completion Dates**
*May 2001–October 2008*

PHOTOGRAPHY BY PUB, SINGAPORE'S
NATIONAL WATER AGENCY (ALL IMAGES)

## DEVELOPMENT TEAM

**Owner/Developer**
City of Sydney
Sydney, New South Wales,
Australia

**Architect**
Tonkin Zulaikha Greer
Sydney, New South Wales,
Australia
www.tzg.com.au

**Landscape Architect**
James Mather Delaney Design
Pty Ltd
Redfern, New South Wales,
Australia
www.jmddesign.com.au

## *Jury* STATEMENT

The site of a former
water reservoir that was
decommissioned in 1899,
Paddington Reservoir
Gardens—with sunken
gardens and ponds,
surrounded by a precast
concrete boardwalk—is the
preservation of a "civic ruin"
in Sydney, returning a site
of heritage significance to
use for the first time in 140
years and offering much-
needed open space in a
dense urban district.

# PADDINGTON RESERVOIR GARDENS, Sydney, Australia

Paddington Reservoir Gardens is a reimagination of a former water reservoir in Sydney, Australia, that was decommissioned in 1899.

A team of designers, led by Sydney-based Tonkin Zulaikha Greer, was commissioned by the Sydney City Council to transform the disused site of the long-crumbled reservoir into a modern urban park. The city anticipated that the new park would replace the subterranean infrastructure. But instead of simply capping the reservoir ruins and building open space on top, the designers used the existing structure to create a public space that seamlessly merges Sydney's past and present.

Completed in 1878, the original Paddington Reservoir was designed by Sydney's city engineer, Edward Bell. It was an important element in the city's water distribution system and served the growing population well until the turn of the century. Later, it was kept as a maintenance facility by the Metropolitan Water, Sewerage and Drainage Board and then was leased as a commercial parking garage with grassed open space at street level until 1990 when some of the reservoir's original vaults collapsed, forcing its closure.

In 2006, work began to reinvent the facility into a public space that could serve the needs of modern Sydney. Upon visiting the reservoir, project designers were struck by the beauty of the "municipal ruins" and chose to create a park that honors the site's rich heritage by opening and exposing the underground building and weaving green courtyards throughout the site to create the two-tiered Paddington Reservoir Gardens.

The new park is located in the dense downtown area of Sydney's Paddington neighborhood in a civic zone near the Paddington Town Hall; Juniper Hall, a historic landmark; and the post office, providing much-needed open space. The park also has a palpable and functional connection with the town hall, because the gardens are irrigated with rainwater collected from the hall's roof, which is then stored underground. Within the green areas of the sunken park, both public performances and more casual gatherings can be accommodated. The park has been crowded with people since its opening last year.

To honor the site's past, designers retained all materials from the original structure and used them to create dramatic spaces and plays of light across what remained of the historic vaults and walls. The variety of new materials was kept to a minimum. Only steel, aluminum, and concrete were used to create the park's new features, which include walkways and access points from street level, all of which mimic the distinctive curves of the brick vaults. Two roofs over the entry to the park's lower level echo the shape of the vaults below, creating a connection between street level and the expanse below that beckons visitors to the new space.

Paddington Reservoir Gardens is also a true garden. Historically accurate plantings were chosen to evoke the Victorian era of the structure's birth, and the park is divided into "rooms" that create intimate garden spaces that are in stark contrast to the vast open spaces that predominate in Sydney. The sunken subtropical garden is set in ruins along with a constructed pond that has been referred to as a "lake of contemplation."

This space is a new model for adaptive use and preservation of heritage in dense urban areas, creating a reminder of the relatively recent past while also providing a respite from city life. By injecting a long-forgotten piece of municipal infrastructure with new life through strategic structural and landscape design interventions, a thoroughly modern public space has emerged.

## PROJECT DATA

**Web Site**
www.tzg.com.au/projects/
paddington-reservoir

**Site Area**
0.35 ha (0.86 ac)

**Facilities**
3,500 m² (37,670 sf)

**Land Use**
park/open space

**Start/Completion Dates**
2006–March 2009

PHOTOGRAPHY BY BRETT BOARDMAN; ERIC SIERENS (80)
CITY OF SYDNEY; FIORA SACCO (82)
CITY OF SYDNEY; BRETT BOARDMAN (83)

## The Americas Jury

**Marty Jones, Jury Chair**
*Boston, Massachusetts*

Marty Jones is president and CEO of MassDevelopment, the quasi-public finance and development authority of Massachusetts. Previously the president of Boston building, development, and property management company Corcoran Jennison, Jones has spent decades in the real estate industry. She got her start at the U.S. Department of Housing and Urban Development in both the Washington and Boston offices.

At Corcoran Jennison, Jones managed staff and project teams for new development projects that transformed communities, directed asset management for multifamily portfolios, chaired a joint venture between Corcoran Jennison and Beacon Communities, and directed all aspects of the Westminster Company, a 175-employee operation with 66 properties and 5,000 apartment units in North and South Carolina.

Jones graduated from Brown University.

**Michael Balaban**
*Washington, D.C.*

Michael Balaban is president of Lowe Enterprises Real Estate Group, Eastern Region, with overall responsibility for commercial property investment, development, and management activities in the region. Previously, Balaban was the acquisitions officer of the Washington Real Estate Investment Trust. Prior to that, he was a Massachusetts-registered architect and real estate consultant active in the New England area.

Balaban received a bachelor's degree from Kenyon College, a master's in architecture at Harvard Graduate School of Design, and a master's of business administration from the University of Pennsylvania.

## Greg Baldwin
*Portland, Oregon*

Greg Baldwin, a partner at Zimmer Gunsul Frasca Architects LP (ZGF) in Portland, passed away June 25, 2011, at age 70. Much of his career was influenced by his commitment to integrate urban design and architecture through cooperative public/private partnerships. Several of his projects, perhaps most notably Portland's MAX Light Rail system, have become models for other cities nationally. He designed complex building projects across the country—office and mixed-use developments, historic and adaptive use, academic and performance facilities, and transit systems—with clients who have been aggressive in their efforts to enhance the livability of their communities.

A Fellow of the American Institute of Architects and the American Academy in Rome, Baldwin received a BA, a master's of architecture, and a master's of architecture in urban design from Harvard University, as well as a Marshall Prize and Fulbright Fellowship for his postgraduate studies. He was also the recipient of a Rome Prize in Architecture at the American Academy. Following his European studies, he worked for Skidmore Owings & Merrill in Portland and renovated facilities for Portland Public Schools before joining ZGF in 1979, and becoming a partner in 1985, where he remained until his death.

Baldwin was not afraid to push various assumptions, principles, or processes to build a better, more compelling, livable, and resilient outcome. He enriched those who were touched by his extraordinary wisdom, gentle nature, and clear vision of the art of the possible. His practice leaves a lasting legacy on Portland, the region, and the country.

## Douglas Betz
*Dayton, Ohio*

Douglas Betz serves as a senior vice president of Woolpert, Inc., a national architecture, engineering, and planning firm of 750 people. Betz directs a national practice that focuses on the design of theme parks, resorts, industrial/office parks, correctional facilities, master-planned communities, large design/build projects for the U.S. Department of Defense, and retail.

An active member of ULI, Betz has served on several advisory services panels and project analysis teams; he is a member of the Community Retail Council (CRC Green Flight). He has also authored articles for *Urban Land* magazine. Also active in the International Council of Shopping Centers, Betz holds leadership positions at local and state levels. He has been most active in lobbying efforts on behalf of the real estate industry. He currently sits on the board of a community performing arts organization and an educational foundation.

A graduate of the University of Cincinnati, Betz received a bachelor's degree in urban planning and design.

## Amanda Burden
*New York, New York*

Amanda Burden is chair of the New York City Planning Commission and director of the New York Department of City Planning. Her commitment to making the public realm a focal point of land use planning is apparent throughout New York, including such notable projects as the High Line, an abandoned elevated rail line in Manhattan that the city has started transforming into a unique elevated linear park. More than 30 projects, many by world-renowned architects, have been catalyzed by the plan.

Burden received a BA at Sarah Lawrence College and an MS in urban planning at Columbia University Graduate School of Architecture. In 2009, she was chosen as the winner of the Urban Land Institute's J.C. Nichols Prize for Visionaries in Urban Development, its highest honor for an individual. The prize comes with a $100,000 honorarium, which Burden donated to ULI to create an annual prize to honor transformative and exciting public urban open spaces.

## William Gilchrist
*New Orleans, Louisiana*

In August 2010, William Gilchrist was appointed director of place-based planning for the city of New Orleans by Mayor Mitch Landrieu. From 1993 to 2009, he was director of the Department of Planning, Engineering, and Permits for Birmingham, Alabama. Among other civic and professional groups, the American Institute of Architects (AIA), the American Planning Association, and the National League of Cities have honored the work of his Birmingham department.

A graduate of Massachusetts Institute of Technology (MIT)'s schools of management and architecture, with a master's degree from each, as well as a degree from Harvard's Kennedy School of Government, Gilchrist was among the first Aga Khan traveling fellows, documenting the Swahili architecture of coastal Kenya. He has chaired the committee that oversees the AIA Regional/Urban Design Assistance Teams and is a trustee of the Urban Land Institute as well as vice chairman of its executive committee. Currently, Gilchrist serves on the departmental visiting committee of the MIT School of Architecture.

Gilchrist has been interviewed on National Public Radio, has appeared on PBS's *The News Hour with Jim Lehrer*, and speaks often on urbanism, regional planning, citizen participation in the public realm, and the history of urban settlement.

### Kenneth Hughes
*Dallas, Texas*

Ken Hughes is chief executive officer of Hughes Development, a Dallas-based real estate development firm. Hughes began his career with the Henry S. Miller Company in Dallas. He was with the company for 15 years, eventually becoming executive vice president and a member of the board of directors. He has served as an adviser to several foreign-based developers including Arquitectos Javier Sordo Madaleno on Moliere 333 in Mexico City; Fabrikasa in Caracas, Venezuela; and Lensworth, in Melbourne, Australia.

Hughes has served on the board of directors of the Real Estate Council in Dallas, and he served for three years on the mayor of Dallas's Inside the Loop Committee for the rebuilding of downtown Dallas. He is a continuing guest lecturer on urban housing and mixed-use development with the Real Estate Initiative at the Harvard Graduate School of Design. A member or a leader in several professional and civic organizations, he has been a trustee of the Urban Land Institute and chairman of its *The Dollars and Cents of Shopping Centers*. He currently is on the Policy and Practice Committee of ULI and is a governor of the institute.

Hughes attended the University of Texas at Austin School of Architecture and Southern Methodist University Cox School of Business and has been a member of the advisory board of the Cox School of Business and the Meadows School of the Arts, Southern Methodist University. He currently serves on and is a Life Member of the Advisory Council of the University of Texas at Austin School of Architecture.

### Mark Johnson
*Denver, Colorado*

Mark Johnson is principal of the Denver-based landscape architecture firm Civitas. Johnson has 35 years of experience leading the design of public places. Current work includes the design of Museum Park Miami, the San Diego North Embarcadero, the San Diego Convention Center expansion, the Harlem River Waterfront in upper Manhattan, and a new plaza in downtown Salt Lake City.

Johnson has won many awards for design, planning, and service for his work and influence on the role of landscape architecture in improving cities. He is a frequent lecturer at universities; faculty member for the ULI Daniel Rose Fellowship in Detroit; faculty at the International Academy of Design and Health, Stockholm; and a core member of the Working Group on Sustainable Cities at Harvard. He received his master's of urban design from Harvard University and a bachelor's of landscape architecture from Utah State University.

### Christopher Kurz
*Baltimore, Maryland*

Chris Kurz, the president of Linden Associates, has more than 30 years of commercial real estate experience. Linden Associates, Inc., is a mid-Atlantic-based real estate company that specializes in the development, acquisition, management, and financing of commercial properties from Philadelphia, Pennsylvania, to Raleigh, North Carolina. After graduating from the Wharton School MBA program in 1971, Kurz worked for the Rouse Company. Since 1986, he has operated his own company and has developed over 950,000 square feet of office, retail, and industrial property in the Washington/Baltimore market. During his career, Kurz has developed or acquired over 2,300,000 square feet of commercial real estate and has arranged financing of approximately $750 million.

Between his tenure at Rouse and starting his development company in 1986, Kurz worked for a bank, mortgage banker, and investment banking firm specializing in real estate. As a principal in the real estate affiliate of Alex. Brown & Sons (now Deutsche Bank), he represented public pension fund clients in the financing and acquisition of commercial real estate throughout the United States. He was also responsible for the firm's marketing program to pension funds. As the Baltimore regional manager for H.G. Smithy Co., Kurz represented the real estate departments of Travelers, Manulife, and other insurance companies in the Baltimore and Washington markets. He was hired from Rouse by a regional bank in the mid-1970s to work out a portfolio of troubled assets.

**David Malmuth**
*San Diego, California*

David Malmuth established David Malmuth Development, a real estate development firm focused on the creation of art-inspired places that transform communities, in 2010. Before starting his own firm, Malmuth was the founder and managing director for seven years with RCLCO's Development Services Group. Malmuth drew upon his 25 years of experience in the development business, which included completion as principal developer of over $1 billion in high-profile projects, to assist numerous clients in the planning and execution of mixed-use, entertainment, and waterfront developments. Clients included Rockefeller Group, Kamehameha Schools, MGM MIRAGE, and the sponsor of the "Imagine Coney" charette, the Municipal Art Society.

From 1996 to 2002, Malmuth was a senior vice president at TrizecHahn Development Corporation. Before TrizecHahn, he was vice president/general manager at Disney Development Company–West. During his nine years at the Walt Disney Company, Malmuth managed the development of over $200 million in projects, including the Feature Animation Building in Burbank (with architect Robert Stern) and Disney Ice in Anaheim (with architect Frank Gehry).

Malmuth received his MBA from Stanford University and his BA from Claremont McKenna College. He is a member of the Urban Land Institute's Policy and Practice Committee and a founding board member of Disney Goals, a nonprofit entity that provides underserved Anaheim youth with positive options through sports, academic training, and community service.

**Jeff Mayer**
*Irvine, California*

Jeff Mayer recently completed his third year as chairman of the ULI Orange County/Inland Empire District Council. In professional practice, he leads his own planning and design firm, Jeff Mayer & Partners, with experience across multiple market sectors, including commercial, residential, mixed use, resort, and entertainment. Mayer has gained 30 years of experience as a principal at several major design firms, including CRSS, EDAW, and Gensler.

Mayer's company is currently providing urban design and landscape architecture services to Greentown China on two city blocks in the Ben Hai New CBD of Tianjin, China, and conceptual site planning for two hotels in a new destination resort near Cartagena, Spain. Project awards received include a 2007 Best Community Development Award from the AIA San Fernando Valley for Ritter Ranch.

Mayer has participated on panels at national events for ULI, including the Reinventing Retail and Placemaking Conferences. His work has been published in *AIA Architect*, *Interior Design*, and *Entertainment Design*. In addition to his work with ULI, Mayer is an international board member of the Themed Entertainment Association, which represents creators of compelling places and experiences for his clients such as Disney, Paramount and Universal. This serves as an outlet for his passion for place making and creating exceptional customer experiences.

Mayer holds a BS in planning and landscape architecture from the University of Virginia and undertook graduate study at the University of Pennsylvania's Wharton School of Business.

**Raj Menda**
*Bangalore, India*

Raj Menda is the managing director of RMZ Corp, a leading commercial and residential real estate company in India. RMZ, founded in 2002 by Menda and his family, has developed more than 1.2 million square meters of Class A office space in Bangalore, Hyderabad, Chennai, Kolkata, and Pune. Its first green building was the first office building in India to receive a LEED-Platinum certification. At RMZ, Menda is responsible for sourcing funds, striking deals, and developing and managing office, residential, retail, and hospitality properties.

Menda earned a graduate degree in commerce and business management. He is the honorary secretary of the National Real Estate Developers Association, which is a constituent part of the Confederation of Real Estate Developers Association of India, past Honorary Secretary of the National Confederation of Real Estate Developers Association of India, in 2009 chairman of the ULI Asia Pacific Awards, an active member of the Global Real Estate Institute and the Urban Land Institute, and a founding member of the Bangalore chapter of the Young Presidents' Organization.

**Luca de Ambrosis Ortigara**
*Milan, Italy*

Luca de Ambrosis Ortigara is chief executive officer (CEO) and partner of DEA Real Estate Advisor, which focuses on high-level retail premises, commercial services, and strategic advisory services for prime customers' property assets. He is also a founding partner of Realty Partners, an Italian real estate management and strategic advisory firm (2004) focusing on five areas: strategic consulting, asset management, real estate fund management, commercial services, and equity investment. Among its clients are Credit Suisse, Caisse de Dépôt et Placement du Québec, First Boston, Gruppo Fondiaria, Aedes, Pirelli RE, and Deka. Previously, he worked with McArthurGlen as CEO for Italy and group commercial director for Europe. He has also worked at Pirelli Real Estate as director of real estate services and was a partner in Cushman and Wakefield.

Ortigara is chair of Urban Land Institute Italy and a member of the executive committee of MAPIC. He also sits on the Scientific and Retail Executive Committee of Expo Italia Real Estate. He has been a visiting professor for the master's degree course in Fashion, Experience, and Design at the SDA Bocconi University in Milan.

# Asia Pacific Jury

## Ross Holt, Jury Chair
*Perth, Australia*

Ross Holt is chief executive of LandCorp, a government trading enterprise that operates as the Western Australia government's specialist property development agency. LandCorp provides a commercially oriented vehicle for delivering the state's strategic land development goals.

LandCorp's professional staff provides a diverse set of property development services, including property acquisition and planning, business administration, and strategic marketing, helping LandCorp operate with a triple-bottom-line approach. Over half of its more than 200 projects throughout the state are located outside the capital city of Perth.

Under Holt's leadership, LandCorp has focused on sustainable development outcomes for the benefit of the affected community. It has sought to extend those outcomes to the built form through the application of design and building guidelines and through joint ventures with private sector development and building entities.

Holt graduated from the University of Western Australia with an honors degree in economics. Prior to joining LandCorp in 1993, he held a senior position in the state's treasury department.

## Albert Chan
*Shanghai, China*

Albert Chan is the director of development planning and design at Shui On Land, the flagship property development company of the Shui On Group in China, and has a track record in developing large-scale, mixed-use city-core redevelopment projects. Listed in Hong Kong and based in Shanghai, Shui On Group has eight projects in various stages of development in prime locations of major cities, with a land bank of 13.1 million square meters.

Chan joined Shui On in 1997 in Shanghai and has more than 25 years of experience in planning, design, and real estate development. He manages the conceptualization, site feasibility studies, master planning, and design of award-winning developments for Shui On in Shanghai, Wuhan, Chongqing, Foshan, and Dalian. From 1997 to 2001, he led the planning and design effort for Shanghai Xintiandi, an adaptive use development widely regarded as a landmark in China;

it became the first development in China to receive a ULI Award for Excellence. He also focuses on new product development and product standardization, and chairs the Sustainable Development Committee at the company, which has so far received LEED-ND certification for three master-planned communities and other LEED certification/precertification for 12 projects.

Before joining Shui On, Chan worked at the New York City Department of Design and Construction and at Cooper, Robertson + Partners. His education includes an MS in urban design from Columbia University, an MArch from the University of California at Berkeley, and an MBA from New York University. He is a registered architect of New York state.

## Mark Fogle
*Hong Kong, China*

Mark Fogle is the managing director for Asia Pacific Infrastructure and chief investment officer of RREEF Asia, based in Singapore. Fogle joined RREEF in 2007 and has more than 25 years of asset management and investment experience, 15 of which have been spent in the Asia Pacific region. RREEF has about $62.4 billion in assets under management globally and focuses on investments in real estate, infrastructure, and private equity. RREEF Asia's real estate business has about $1.6 billion in assets under management.

From 1997 to 2006, Fogle was a managing director of AIG Global Investment Corp., the investment arm of American International Group, Inc. Prior to joining AIG, he was responsible for the Asian expansion of the John Buck Company, a U.S. development and service firm.

## Fun Siew Leng
*Singapore*

As group director (urban planning and design) in the Urban Redevelopment Authority of Singapore, Fun Siew Leng oversees the planning and urban design for the Central Area. Her responsibilities include the formulation of strategic long-term plans, detailed urban design plans, and policies. She also oversees the work of the Marina Bay Development Agency, which promotes and markets Marina Bay.

Fun chairs the Design Advisory Panel (DAP) for key projects in the Central Area to guide the design development of these projects. She is a member of the DAP for the Proposed Sports Hub Development and the National Art Gallery project. She was recently appointed to sit on the

Steering Committee for the Restoration and Refurbishment of Victoria Theatre/Victoria Concert Hall and the new Singapore Science Centre. She sits on the Board of Architects and the Land Transport Authority's Architectural Design Review Panel, as well as the Public Utilities Board's ABC Waters Review Panel. She is also a member of the Singapore Tourism Board Organising Committee for the World Expo 2010 in Shanghai.

A registered architect with 23 years of experience, Fun obtained her master's of architecture in urban design from Harvard University in 1993. Prior to joining the Urban Redevelopment Authority, she amassed 13 years of experience in public housing design with the Housing & Development Board, Singapore.

## Keith Griffiths
*Hong Kong, China*

Keith Griffiths studied architecture at St. John's College, Cambridge University, and has practiced architecture for three decades. He formed his architectural practice in Hong Kong in 1985 and led the company into the creation of Aedas in 2001. He has overseen the phenomenal growth of Aedas to become the world's second-largest architectural practice with 40 offices worldwide.

Griffiths has a well-recognized reputation for outstanding leadership and innovation. He is a recognized and sought-after designer who promotes sustainable design excellence and cultural integration as the keystones of Aedas's philosophy. He facilitates international design workshops, reviews, staff training, and educational outreach programs and is an instigator and champion of Aedas's integration into the many communities, cultures, and countries the company works with. Griffiths provides a driving force in Aedas's work to improve the environment through the built form and its integration into the fabric of our communities.

## Paul Husband
*Hong Kong, China*

Paul Husband is managing director of Husband Retail Consulting, a global consulting firm with experience in innovative retail center planning, place making, marketing, and leasing for international clients wishing to maximize their retail asset growth. Husband Retail Consulting has more than ten years of global and Asia-specific experience working with international real estate developers on successful iconic projects and luxury shopping centers worldwide. A native of the United Kingdom, Husband launched his career as marketing manager for Pacific Place in Hong Kong, one of Asia's most successful and high-profile retail centers.

Husband is also an Asian faculty member of the International Council of Shopping Centers and a member of the Washington-based Urban Land Institute and is frequently invited to speak at key conferences and seminars around the world, particularly in relation to future luxury retail trends across China, India, and throughout Asia. In 2006, he made his debut as an author, with the launch of *The Cult of the Luxury Brand*.

## Hokyu Lee
*Seoul, Korea*

Hokyu Lee was appointed chairman of Savills Korea in July 2009. Before taking a role as chairman, Lee was appointed as both Savills Asia Pacific Executive Member in 2006 and Representative of Savills Korea and was responsible for overseeing Korea's operations comprising some 150 staff in two cities, Seoul and Busan.

In 1994, Lee founded BHP Korea as the first international property-consulting firm in Korea, providing a comprehensive scope of services related to all aspects of real estate development, investment, transactions, operation, valuation, asset management, and marketing and overseas investment. In 1999, Lee also founded Korea Asset Advisors, a real estate asset management company. The company was a leader in the market, managing 27 properties with more than 1 million square meters under its property and asset management with leasing-marketing.

Lee graduated from Columbia University with a master's of architecture in urban design in 1988.

## Tomohisa Miyauchi
*Tokyo, Japan*

Tomohisa Miyauchi is a partner at ISSHO Architects, a Tokyo design firm that he cofounded after graduating from the Harvard Graduate School of Design and the Southern California Institute of Architecture. The firm designs a large variety of projects, including houses, apartments, offices, boutiques, hotels, and mixed-use spaces. The firm works both locally in Tokyo and increasingly abroad, with projects in China, such as a pavilion at the 2010 Shanghai Expo and a fashion boutique.

Miyauchi is responsible for representing the company; interacting with clients, among whom are developers and landowners; and collaborating with professionals from different fields. He also developed ISSHO's philosophy of humanistic architecture, focusing on personal involvement in community on both neighborhood and global levels and collaboration between diverse experts. He belongs to the Tokyo Society of Architects & Building Engineers and the American Institute of Architects and is a senior editor of *Architecture + Urbanism* magazine.

## Rita Soh
*Singapore*

Rita Soh was elected president, Board of Architects Singapore, as of January 2010, for a term of three years and is also currently serving a second term as a board member in the Singapore Land Authority. She was the deputy chairman, zone B, of the Architects Regional Council of Asia (ARCASIA) from 2008 to 2010.

Soh was the president of the Singapore Institute of Architects from 2004 to 2007 and was instrumental in establishing a blueprint for the architectural profession in its pursuit of architectural excellence as well as a pro-enterprise approach in architecture.

To champion Asian architecture, Soh, with Getz, launched the biannual SIA-Getz Architecture Prize for Emergent Architecture in Asia in 2005. She was a jury member in the Design Evaluation Panels for the Integrated Resorts at Marina Bay & Sentosa Island, the Gardens by the Bay design competition, the Singapore Sports Hub as well as the National Art Gallery. She was also a jury member for the Inaugural President's Design of the Year and Designer of the Year in 2006, 2007, and again in 2010.

## Rocco Yim
*Hong Kong, China*

Rocco Yim founded his own practice in 1979 and was one of the cofounders of Rocco Design Partners in 1982. The firm has received many local and international awards and citations for design excellence since its inception and won its first international competition in 1983. Recent accolades include ARCASIA Gold Medals in 1994 and 2003, the Chicago Athenaeum Architectural Award in 2006, the Kenneth F. Brown Award in 2007, and winning designs through international competitions for the Guangdong Museum in 2004 and the Hong Kong special administrative region Government Headquarters at Tamar in 2007. Under his stewardship in design, the firm has grown significantly over the years in both size and reputation. Yim is also an honorary professor at the Hong Kong University Department of Architecture and a museum adviser to the Leisure and Cultural Services Department of Hong Kong.

Yim is regularly invited to speak at international symposia and seminars, such as the ARCASIA Forum, the IAA Symposia, and the Harvard Graduate School of Design Conference and New Trends Architecture 2005. His work has been published in such regional and international journals as *SD, SPACE, AR, Zoo, ROOT, Domus, Frames, Art in America*, and *Architectural Review*. He graduated from the University of Hong Kong in 1979.

# PAST ULI AWARDS FOR EXCELLENCE WINNERS

The following 310 projects have received ULI Awards for Excellence. Each project name is followed by its location and its developer/owner.

**1979**
*First year of award*
The Galleria; Houston, Texas; Hines Interests Limited Partnership

**1980**
Charles Center; Baltimore, Maryland; Baltimore City Development Corporation

**1981**
WDW/Reedy Creek; Orlando, Florida; The Walt Disney Company

**1982**
*Two awards given: large and small scale*
Large Scale: Heritage Village; Southbury, Connecticut; Heritage Development Group, Inc.
Small Scale: Promontory Point; Newport Beach, California; The Irvine Company

**1983**
Large Scale: Eaton Centre; Toronto, Canada; Cadillac Fairview Limited

**1984**
Large Scale: Embarcadero Center; San Francisco, California; Embarcadero Center, Ltd.
Small Scale: Rainbow Centre; Niagara Falls, New York; The Cordish Company

**1985**
*Introduction of product categories*
New Community: Las Colinas; Irving, Texas; JPI Partners, Inc.
• Large-Scale Residential: Museum Tower; New York, New York; The Charles H. Shaw Company • Small-Scale Urban Mixed Use: Sea Colony Condominiums; Santa Monica, California; Dominion Property Company • Large-Scale Recreational: Sea Pines Plantation; Hilton Head, South Carolina; Community Development Institute • Small-Scale Urban Mixed Use: Vista Montoya; Los Angeles, California; Pico Union Neighborhood Council/Community Redevelopment Agency

**1986**
*Introduction of rehabilitation and special categories*
Small-Scale Mixed Use: 2000 Pennsylvania Avenue; Washington, D.C.; George Washington University • Small-Scale Rehabilitation: Downtown Costa Mesa; Costa Mesa, California; PSB Realty Corporation • Special: Inner Harbor Shoreline; Baltimore, Maryland; Baltimore City Development Corporation • Large-Scale Recreational: Kaanapali Beach

Resort; Kaanapali, Hawaii; Amfac/JMB Hawaii • Large-Scale Residential: The Landings on Skidaway Island; Savannah, Georgia; The Bramigar Organization, Inc. • Small-Scale Industrial/Office Park: The Purdue Frederick Company; Norwalk, Connecticut; The Purdue Frederick Company • Large-Scale Recreational: Water Tower Place; Chicago, Illinois; JMB Realty Corporation

## 1987
Large-Scale Industrial/Office Park: Bishop Ranch Business Park; San Ramon, California; Sunset Development Company • Small-Scale Commercial/Retail: Loews Ventana Canyon Resort; Tucson, Arizona; Estes Homebuilding • Large-Scale Urban Mixed Use: St. Louis Union Station; St. Louis, Missouri; The Rouse Company • Small-Scale Residential: Straw Hill; Manchester, New Hampshire; George Matarazzo and Mark Stebbins • Rehabilitation: The Willard Inter-Continental; Washington, D.C.; The Oliver Carr Company

## 1988
Large-Scale Urban Mixed Use: Copley Place; Boston, Massachusetts; Urban Investment & Development Company • Special: Downtown Women's Center; Los Angeles, California; The Ratkovitch Company • Large-Scale Commercial/Retail: The Grand Avenue; Milwaukee, Wisconsin; Milwaukee Redevelopment Corporation (MRC) • Rehabilitation: Northpoint; Chicago, Illinois; Amoco Neighborhood Development • Small-Scale Residential: Pickleweed Apartments; Mill Valley, California; BRIDGE Housing Corporation • Large-Scale Residential: Rector Place; New York, New York; Battery Park City Authority • Small-Scale Office: Wilshire Palisades; Santa Monica, California; Tooley & Company

## 1989
*Introduction of Heritage Award*
Small-Scale Urban Mixed Use: Charleston Place; Charleston, South Carolina; The Taubman Company, Inc., and Cordish Embry Associates (joint venture) • Rehabilitation: Commonwealth Development; Boston, Massachusetts; Corcoran Management • Small-Scale Office: Escondido City Hall; Escondido, California; City of Escondido • Large-Scale Office: Norwest Center; Minneapolis, Minnesota; Hines Interests • Special: Pratt-Willert Neighborhood; Buffalo, New York; City of Buffalo • New Community: Reston; Reston, Virginia; Mobil Land Development in Virginia • **Heritage Award: Rockefeller Center**; New York, New York; The Rockefeller Group • Large-Scale Urban Mixed Use: Rowes Wharf; Boston, Massachusetts; The Beacon Companies

## 1990
Small-Scale Commercial: The Boulders; Carefree, Arizona; Westcor Partners • Large-Scale Industrial: Carnegie Center; Princeton, New Jersey; Carnegie Center Associates • Small-Scale Residential: Columbia Place; San Diego, California; Odmark & Thelan • Large-Scale Residential:

River Run; Boise, Idaho; O'Neill Enterprises, Inc. • Special: Tent City; Boston, Massachusetts; Tent City Corporation • Rehabilitation: Wayne County Building; Detroit, Michigan; Farbman Stein • New Community: Woodlake; Richmond, Virginia; East West Partners of Virginia

## 1991
Small-Scale Commercial/Retail: Del Mar Plaza; Del Mar, California; Del Mar Partnership • Large-Scale Urban Mixed Use: Fashion Centre at Pentagon City; Arlington, Virginia; Melvin Simon & Associates and Rose Associates • Small-Scale Urban Mixed Use: Garibaldi Square; Chicago, Illinois; The Charles H. Shaw Company • Large-Scale Residential: Ghent Square; Norfolk, Virginia; Norfolk Redevelopment and Housing Authority • Special: Grand Central Partnership; New York, New York; Grand Central Partnership • Small-Scale Office: James R. Mills Building; San Diego, California; Starboard Development Corporation • Rehabilitation: Marina Village; Alameda, California; Vintage Properties • Special: Union Station; Washington, D.C.; Union Station Redevelopment Corporation

## 1992
Small-Scale Commercial/Retail: CocoWalk; Miami, Florida; Constructa U.S. • Special: The Coeur d'Alene Resort Golf Course; Coeur d'Alene, Idaho; Hagadone Hospitality • Special: The Delancey Street Foundation; San Francisco, California; The Delancey Street Foundation • Public: Harbor Point; Boston, Massachusetts; Corcoran Jennison Companies • Large-Scale Mixed Use: Market Square; Washington, D.C.; Trammell Crow • New Community: Planned Community of Mission Viejo; Mission Viejo, California; Mission Viejo Company • Small-Scale Residential: Summit Place; St. Paul, Minnesota; Robert Engstrom Companies • Rehabilitation: Tysons Corner Center; McLean, Virginia; The L&B Group

## 1993
Small-Scale Residential: Beverly Hills Senior Housing; Beverly Hills, California; Jewish Federation Council • Special: Charlestown Navy Yard; Charlestown, Massachusetts; Boston Redevelopment Authority • **Heritage Award: The Country Club Plaza**; Kansas City, Missouri; J.C. Nichols Company • Large-Scale Residential: The Cypress of Hilton Head Island; Hilton Head Island, South Carolina; The Melrose Company • Small-Scale Rehabilitation: Furness House; Baltimore, Maryland; The Cordish Company • Large-Scale Recreational: Kapalua; Kapalua, Maui, Hawaii; Kapalua Land Company, Ltd. • Special: Post Office Square Park and Garage; Boston, Massachusetts; Friends of Post Office Square, Inc. • Rehabilitation: Schlitz Park; Milwaukee, Wisconsin; The Brewery Works, Inc. • Small-Scale Commercial/Retail: The Somerset Collection; Troy, Michigan; Forbes/Cohen Properties and Frankel Associates

## 1994

*Introduction of international category*

International: Broadgate; London, United Kingdom; Stanhope Properties • Small-Scale Residential: Orchard Village; Chattanooga, Tennessee; Chattanooga Neighborhood Enterprise • Public: Oriole Park at Camden Yards; Baltimore, Maryland; Maryland Stadium Authority • Special: The Pennsylvania Avenue Plan; Washington, D.C.; Pennsylvania Avenue Development Corporation • Large-Scale Rehabilitation: Phipps Plaza; Atlanta, Georgia; Compass Retail, Inc. • **Heritage Award: Sea Pines Plantation**; Hilton Head Island, South Carolina; Charles Fraser • Large-Scale Office: Washington Mutual Tower; Seattle, Washington; Wright Runstad and Company • Large-Scale Residential: Woodbridge; Irvine, California; The Irvine Company • Special: The Woodlands; The Woodlands, Texas; The Woodlands Corporation

## 1995

Small-Scale Rehabilitation: 640 Memorial Drive; Cambridge, Massachusetts; Massachusetts Institute of Technology Real Estate • Large-Scale Commercial/Retail: Broadway Plaza; Walnut Creek, California; Macerich Northwestern Associates and The Macerich Company • **Heritage Award: Disneyland Park**; Anaheim, California; The Walt Disney Company • Large-Scale Industrial/Office: Irvine Spectrum; Orange County, California; The Irvine Company • Small-Scale Recreational: Little Nell Hotel and Aspen Mountain Base; Aspen, Colorado; Aspen Skiing Company • Special: Monterey Bay Aquarium; Monterey, California; The Monterey Bay Aquarium Foundation • New Community: Pelican Bay; Naples, Florida; WCI Communities LP • Special: Riverbank State Park; New York, New York; New York State Office of Parks, Recreation and Historic Preservation • Small-Scale Residential: Strathern Park Apartments; Sun Valley, California; Thomas Safran and Associates

## 1996

Large-Scale Residential: Avenel; Potomac, Maryland; Natelli Communities • Public: Bryant Park; New York, New York; Bryant Park Restoration Corporation • Large-Scale Office: Comerica Tower at Detroit Center; Detroit, Michigan; Hines Interests Limited Partnership • Small-Scale Residential: The Court Home Collection at Valencia NorthPark; Valencia, California; The Newhall Land and Farming Company, and RGC • Small-Scale Commercial/Hotel: The Forum Shops; Las Vegas, Nevada; Simon Property Group • Small-Scale Mixed Use: The Heritage on the Garden; Boston, Massachusetts; The Druker Company • Large-Scale Recreational: Kiawah Island; Kiawah Island, South Carolina; Kiawah Resort Associates LP • Special: The Scattered Site Program; Chicago, Illinois; The Habitat Company

## 1997

**Heritage Award: The Arizona Biltmore Hotel and Resort**; Phoenix, Arizona; Grossman Company Properties • Rehabilitation: Chelsea Piers; New York, New York; Chelsea Piers LP • Large-Scale Recreational: Desert Mountain; Scottsdale, Arizona; Desert Mountain Properties • Rehabilitation: Eagles Building Restoration; Seattle, Washington; A Contemporary Theater and Housing Resources Group (general partners) • Small-Scale Residential: Mercado Apartments; San Diego, California; City of San Diego Redevelopment Agency • Large-Scale Commercial/Hotel: Park Meadows; Park Meadows, Colorado; TrizecHahn Centers • Special: Pennsylvania Convention Center; Philadelphia, Pennsylvania; Pennsylvania Convention Center Authority • Special: A Safe House for Kids and Moms; Irvine, California; Human Options • Public: Smyrna Town Center; Smyrna, Georgia; City of Smyrna, Knight-Davidson Companies (residential) and Thomas Enterprises (retail/offices) • International: Stockley Park at Heathrow; Uxbridge, Middlesex, United Kingdom; Stanhope Properties PLC

## 1998

Large-Scale Business Park: Alliance; Fort Worth, Texas; Hillwood Development Corporation • Special: American Visionary Art Museum; Baltimore, Maryland; Rebecca and LeRoy E. Hoffberger • International: Calakmul; Mexico City, Mexico; Francisco G. Coronado (owner) • Small-Scale Residential: Courthouse Hill; Arlington, Virginia; Eakin/Youngentob Associates, Inc. • Public: Harold Washington Library Center; Chicago, Illinois; U.S. Equities Realty (developer) • Special: Richmond City Center; Richmond, California; BRIDGE Housing Corporation (owner) • Rehabilitation: Twenty-Eight State Street; Boston, Massachusetts; Equity Office Properties Trust • Rehabilitation: UtiliCorp United World Headquarters/New York Life Building; Kansas City, Missouri; The Zimmer Companies • Small-Scale Recreational: Village Center; Beaver Creek, Colorado; East West Partners

## 1999

Small-Scale Rehabilitation: Bayou Place; Houston, Texas; The Cordish Company • Large-Scale Residential: Bonita Bay; Bonita Springs, Florida; Bonita Bay Properties Inc. • Public: Chicago Public Schools Capital Improvement Program; Chicago, Illinois; Chicago Public Schools • Small-Scale Commercial/Hotel: The Commons at Calabasas; Calabasas, California; Caruso Affiliated Holdings • Special: Coors Field; Denver, Colorado; Denver Metropolitan Stadium District • Small-Scale Mixed Use: East Pointe; Milwaukee, Wisconsin; Milwaukee Redevelopment Corporation and Mandel Group Inc. • Large-Scale Recreational: Hualalai; Ka'upulehu-Kona, Hawaii; Ka'upulehu Makai Venture/Hualalai Development Company • Large-Scale Rehabilitation: John Hancock Center; Chicago, Illinois; U.S. Equities Realty • Small-Scale Residential: Normandie Village; Los Angeles, California; O.N.E. Company Inc. and SIPA (general partners) • Small-Scale Commercial/Hotel: Seventh & Collins Parking Facility (Ballet Valet); Miami Beach, Florida; City of Miami Beach, Goldman Properties • International: Vinohradský Pavilon; Prague, Czech Republic; Prague Investment, a.s.

## 2000

Small-Scale Rehabilitation: Amazon.com Building; Seattle, Washington; Wright Runstad and Company • **Heritage Award: The Burnham Plan**; Chicago, Illinois; The Commercial Club of Chicago • Small-Scale Residential: The Colony; Newport Beach, California; Irvine Apartment Communities • Large-Scale Residential: Coto de Caza; Orange County, California; Lennar Communities • Small-Scale Mixed Use: DePaul Center; Chicago, Illinois; DePaul University • Public: NorthLake Park Community School; Orlando, Florida; Lake Nona Land Company • Large-Scale Rehabilitation: The Power Plant; Baltimore, Maryland; The Cordish Company • International: Sony Center am Potsdamer Platz; Berlin, Germany; Tishman Speyer Properties, Sony Corporation, Kajima Corporation, and BE-ST Development GmbH & Co. (owner) • Special: Spring Island; Beaufort County, South Carolina; Chaffin/Light Associates • Public: The Townhomes on Capitol Hill; Washington, D.C.; Ellen Wilson CDC and Telesis Corporation • Large-Scale Recreational: Whistler Village/Blackcomb Benchlands; Whistler, British Columbia, Canada; Resort Municipality of Whistler, and INTRAWEST Corporation

## 2001

*International category eliminated*

New Community: Celebration; Celebration, Florida; The Celebration Company • Special: Dewees Island; Dewees Island, South Carolina; Island Preservation Partnership • Large-Scale Residential: Harbor Steps; Seattle, Washington; Harbor Properties Inc. • Small-Scale Rehabilitation; Pier 1; San Francisco, California; AMB Property Corporation • Small-Scale Recreational: The Reserve; Indian Wells, California; Lowe Enterprises Inc. • Small-Scale Office: Thames Court; London, United Kingdom; Markborough Properties Limited • Special: Townhomes at Oxon Creek; Washington, D.C.; William C. Smith & Company Inc. • Large-Scale Mixed Use: Valencia Town Center Drive; Valencia, California; The Newhall Land and Farming Company • Large-Scale Commercial/Hotel: The Venetian Casino Resort; Las Vegas, Nevada; LVS/Development Group • Public: Yerba Buena Gardens; San Francisco, California; Yerba Buena Alliance

## 2002

Small-Scale Mixed Use: Bethesda Row; Bethesda, Maryland; Federal Realty Investment Trust • Large-Scale Mixed Use: CityPlace; West Palm Beach, Florida; The Related Companies • Special: Envision Utah; Salt Lake City, Utah; Coalition for Utah's Future • Public: Homan Square Community Center Campus; Chicago, Illinois; Homan Square Community Center Foundation (owner) and The Shaw Company (developer) • Small-Scale Rehabilitation: Hotel Burnham at the Reliance Building; Chicago, Illinois; McCaffery Interests • Special: Memphis Ballpark District; Memphis, Tennessee; Memphis Redbirds Foundation (owner), and Parkway Properties Inc. (developer) • Large-Scale Office: One Raffles Link; Singapore Central, Singapore; Hongkong Land Property Co. Ltd. • Small-Scale Rehabilitation: REI Denver Flagship Store; Denver, Colorado; Recreational Equipment Inc. •

Large-Scale Recreational: Station Mont Tremblant; Quebec, Canada; Intrawest • New Community: Summerlin North; Las Vegas, Nevada; The Rouse Company

## 2003

*Product categories eliminated*

Atago Green Hills; Tokyo, Japan; Mori Building Company • Ayala Center Greenbelt 3; Makati City, Manila, Philippines; Ayala Land Inc. • Bay Harbor; Bay Harbor, Michigan; Victor International Corporation • Chattahoochee River Greenway; Georgia; Chattahoochee River Coordinating Committee • The Grove and Farmers Market; Los Angeles, California; Caruso Affiliated Holdings (The Grove), and A.F. Gilmore Company (Farmers Market) • Millennium Place; Boston, Massachusetts; Millennium Partners/MDA Associates • Shanghai Xintiandi (North Block); Shanghai, China; Shui On Group • The Town of Seaside; Seaside, Florida; Seaside Community Development Corporation • The Villages of East Lake; Atlanta, Georgia; East Lake Community Foundation Inc. • The West Philadelphia Initiatives; Philadelphia, Pennsylvania; University of Pennsylvania

## 2004 The Americas and Asia Pacific

Baldwin Park; Orlando, Florida; Baldwin Park Development Company • Fall Creek Place; Indianapolis, Indiana; City of Indiana (owner), • Mansur Real Estate Services Inc., and King Park Area Development Corporation (developers) • First Ward Place/The Garden District; Charlotte, North Carolina; City of Charlotte (owner), Banc of America Community Development Corporation (master developer) • The Fullerton Square Project; Singapore; Far East Organization/Sino Land • Playhouse Square Center; Cleveland, Ohio; Playhouse Square Foundation • The Plaza at PPL Center; Allentown, Pennsylvania; Liberty Property Trust • Technology Square at Georgia Institute of Technology; Atlanta, Georgia; Georgia Institute of Technology and Georgia Tech Foundation (owners), Jones Lang LaSalle (development manager) • University Park at MIT; Cambridge, Massachusetts; Forest City Enterprises, City of Cambridge Community Development Department, and Massachusetts Institute of Technology • Walt Disney Concert Hall; Los Angeles, California; Los Angeles County (owner), Walt Disney Concert Hall Inc. (developer) • WaterColor; Seagrove Beach, Florida; The St. Joe Company

## 2004 Europe

*Introduction of separate European awards program*

Brindleyplace; Birmingham, United Kingdom; Argent Group PLC • Bullring; Birmingham, United Kingdom; The Birmingham Alliance • Casa de les Punxes; Barcelona, Spain; Inmobiliaria Colonial • Diagonal Mar; Barcelona, Spain; Hines Interests España • Promenaden Hauptbahnhof Leipzig; Leipzig, Germany; ECE Projektmanagement GmbH & Co., Deutsche Bahn AG, and DB Immobilienfonds • Regenboogpark; Tilburg, The Netherlands; AM Wonen

## 2005 The Americas

34th Street Streetscape Program; New York, New York; 34th Street Partnership • 731 Lexington Avenue/One Beacon Court; New York, New York; Vornado Realty Trust • **Heritage Award**: **The Chautauqua Institution**; Chautauqua, New York; The Chautauqua Institution • Fourth Street Live!; Louisville, Kentucky; The Cordish Company • The Glen; Glenview, Illinois; The Village of Glenview and Mesirow Stein Real Estate Inc. • Harbor Town; Memphis, Tennessee; Henry Turley Company and Belz Enterprises • The Market Common, Clarendon; Arlington, Virginia; McCaffery Interests Inc. • **Millennium Park**; Chicago, Illinois; City of Chicago and Millennium Park Inc. • Pueblo del Sol; Los Angeles, California; The Related Companies of California, McCormack Baron Salazar, The Lee Group, and Housing Authority of the City of Los Angeles • Time Warner Center; New York, New York; The Related Companies LP • Ville Plácido Domingo; Acapulco, Mexico; Casas Geo and CIDECO-Anáhuac

## 2005 Europe

Cézanne Saint-Honoré; Paris, France; Société Foncière Lyonnaise and Predica • Danube House; Prague, Czech Republic; Europolis Real Estate Asset • Government Offices Great George Street; London, United Kingdom; Stanhope PLC and Bovis Lend Lease • De Hoftoren; The Hague, The Netherlands; ING Real Estate Development • Meander; Amsterdam, The Netherlands; Het Oosten Kristal and Latei

## 2005 Asia Pacific

*Introduction of separate Asia Pacific awards program*
Federation Square; Melbourne, Australia; Federation Square Management • **Hangzhou Waterfront**; Hangzhou, China; Hangzhou Hubin Commerce & Tourism Company Ltd. • The Loft; Singapore; CapitaLand Residential Ltd. • **Marunouchi Building**; Tokyo, Japan; Mitsubishi Estate Company Ltd. • Pier 6/7, Walsh Bay; Sydney, Australia; Mirvac Group and Transfield Holdings Pty Ltd.

## 2006 The Americas

Belmar; Lakewood, Colorado; Continuum Partners LLC, McStain neighborhoods, and Trammell Crow Residential • Ladera Ranch; Orange County, California; Rancho Mission Viejo and DMB Consolidated Holdings LLC • Los Angeles Unified School District Construction Program; Los Angeles, California; Los Angeles Unified School District • Mesa Arts Center; Mesa, Arizona; Mesa Arts Center • Montage Resort and Spa; Laguna Beach, California; The Athens Group • **Prudential Center Redevelopment**; Boston, Massachusetts; Boston Properties Inc. • Stapleton District 1; Denver, Colorado; Forest City Enterprises • **The Presidio Trust Management Plan**; San Francisco, California; The Presidio Trust • Victoria Gardens; Rancho Cucamonga, California; Forest City Commercial Development and Lewis Group of Companies • Washington Convention Center; Washington, D.C.; Washington Convention Center Authority

## 2006 Europe

**Agbar Tower**; Barcelona, Spain; Layetana Developments • Muziekgebouw aan 't IJ; Amsterdam, The Netherlands; Dienst Maatschappelikjke Ontwikkeling • **New Milan Fair Complex**; Milan, Italy; Fondazione Fiera Milan • Potsdamer Platz Arkaden; Berlin, Germany; ECE Projektmanagement GmbH • Tour CBX; Paris la Défense, France; Tishman Speyer

## 2006 Asia Pacific

Glentrees; Singapore; CapitaLand Residential Singapore • Izumi Garden; Tokyo, Japan; Sumitomo Realty and Development Company Ltd. • Luohu Land Port and Train Station; Shenzhen, China; Shenzhen Municipal Planning Bureau • **Singapore Conservation Programme**; Singapore; Singapore Urban Redevelopment Authority • Wuxi Li Lake Parklands; Wuxi, China; Wuxi Lake District Planning & Construction Leading Team Office

## 2007 The Americas

1180 Peachtree; Atlanta, Georgia; Hines • 2200; Seattle, Washington; Vulcan Inc. • THE ARC; Washington, D.C.; Building Bridges Across the River • Daniel Island; Charleston, South Carolina; The Daniel Island Company • The Gerding Theater at the Armory; Portland, Oregon; Portland Center Stage • **High Point**; Seattle, Washington; Seattle Housing Authority • Highlands' Garden Village; Denver, Colorado; Perry Rose LLC and Jonathan Rose Companies • **King's Lynne**; Lynn, Massachusetts; King's Lynne Residents Council and Corcoran Mullins Jennison Inc. • RAND Corporation Headquarters; Santa Monica, California; The RAND Corporation • San Diego Ballpark Neighborhood Revitalization; San Diego, California; San Diego Padres, JMI Realty Inc., Bosa Development, Cisterra Partners LLC, and Douglas Wilson Companies • **Urban Outfitters Corporate Campus**; Philadelphia, Pennsylvania; Urban Outfitters Inc. (owner) Philadelphia Industrial Development Corporation (developer)

## 2007 Europe

**Manufaktura**; Łódź, Poland; Group Apsys • **Meudon Campus**; Meudon sur Seine, France; Hines • Kanyon; Istanbul, Turkey; Eczacibasi Holding • Petit Palau; Barcelona, Spain; Fundació Orfeó Català-Palau de la Música Catalana • Terminal 4 at Madrid Barajas Airport; Madrid-Barajas, Spain; AENA Aeropuertos Españoles y Navegación Aérea

## 2007 Asia Pacific

The Ecovillage at Currumbin; Currumbin, Queensland, Australia; Landmatters Currumbin Valley Property Ltd. • **Hong Kong Wetland Park**; Hong Kong, China; Architectural Services Department • The Landmark Scheme; Hong Kong, China; Hongkong Land • Nihonbashi Mitsui Tower; Tokyo, Japan; Mitsui Fudosan Co. Ltd. • Roppongi Hills; Tokyo, Japan; Mori Building Co. Ltd.

## 2008 The Americas

**Adidas Village**; Portland, Oregon; adidas-Salomon North America and Winkler Development Corporation • Army Residential Communities Initiative; U.S.A.-wide; U.S. Department of the Army • Atelier|505; Boston, Massachusetts; The Druker Company, Ltd. • Clipper Mill; Baltimore, Maryland; Struever Bros. Eccles & Rouse • Eleven80; Newark, New Jersey; Cogswell Realty Group • General Motors Renaissance Center; Detroit, Michigan; General Motors and Hines • Medinah Temple-Tree Studios; Chicago, Illinois; Friedman Properties, Ltd. • **National Ballet School of Canada/Radio City**; Toronto, Canada; National • Ballet School of Canada and Context Development, Inc. • Overture Center for the Arts; Madison, Wisconsin; Overture Development Corporation • Solara; Poway, California; Community Housing Works

## 2008 Europe

**Kraanspoor**; Amsterdam, The Netherlands; ING Real Estate Development • Meydan Shopping Square; Istanbul, Turkey; METRO Group Asset Management Gmbh & Co. • Stadsfeestzaal; Antwerp, Belgium; Multi Development Belgium nv • Unilever House; London, United Kingdom; Stanhope PLC and Sloane Blackfriars • Val d'Europe Downtown District; Marne la Vallée, France; Euro Disney Associes SCA, Value Retail PLC, Ségécé, and Nexity SA

## 2008 Asia Pacific

**Beijing Finance Street**; Beijing, China; Beijing Financial Street Holding Co., Ltd. • Bras Basah.Bugis; Singapore; Singapore; Urban Redevelopment Authority • Elements at Kowloon Station; Hong Kong, China; MTR Corporation Limited • The Kirinda Project; Kirinda, Sri Lanka; Colliers International Trust • Tokyo Midtown; Tokyo, Japan; Mitsui Fudosan Group

## 2009 The Americas

**Baltimore Inner Harbor**; Baltimore, Maryland; The Mayor, City Council of Baltimore and Charles Center-Inner Harbor Management, Inc. • **California Academy of Sciences**; San Francisco, California; California Academy of Sciences • Comcast Center; Philadelphia, Pennsylvania; Liberty Property Trust • The Cork Factory; Pittsburgh, Pennsylvania; McCaffery Interests, Inc. • DeVries Place; Milpitas, California; Mid-Peninsula Housing Coalition • Heifer International World Headquarters; Little Rock, Arkansas; Heifer International • Kansas City Power & Light District; Kansas City, Missouri; Cordish Company • Kierland Commons; Scottsdale, Arizona; Woodbine Southwest Corporation • **The Rise**; Vancouver, British Columbia, Canada; Grosvenor Americas • UniverCity; Burnaby, British Columbia, Canada; SFU Community Trust • **West Chelsea/High Line Rezoning Plan**; New York, New York; City of New York, Department of Planning

## 2009 EMEA

Akaretler Row Houses/W Hotel; Istanbul, Turkey; Akaretler Turizm Yatirimlari A.Ş. • **American University in Cairo New Campus**; Cairo, Egypt; AUC • Elmpark Green Urban Quarter; Dublin, Ireland; Radora Developments Ltd. • Hilton Tower; Manchester, United Kingdom; The Beetham Organization • Leoben Judicial Complex; Leoben, Austria; BIG Services • Liverpool One; Liverpool, United Kingdom; Grosvenor • Mountain Dwellings; Copenhagen, Denmark; Hoepfner and Danish Oil Company

## 2009 Asia Pacific

Crowne Plaza Changi Airport; Singapore; LaSalle Investment Management; L.C. Development Ltd. • Namba Parks; Osaka, Japan; Nankai Electric Railway Co. Ltd.; Takashimaya Company Ltd. • Seismically Resistant Sustainable Housing; Bagh and Jareed, Pakistan; Article 25 • **Zhongshan Shipyard Park**; Zhongshan, China; City of Zhongshan

## 2010 The Americas

Andares; Guadalajara, Mexico; Desarrolladora Mexicana de Inmuebles S.A. • **Battery Park City Master Plan**; New York, New York; Battery Park City Authority • Bethel Commercial Center; Chicago, Illinois; Bethel New Life • Columbia Heights; Washington, D.C.; The Government of the District of Columbia • Foundry Square; San Francisco, California; Wilson Meany Sullivan • **L.A. LIVE**; Los Angeles, California; AEG • Madison at 14th Apartments; Oakland, California; Affordable Housing Associates • Sundance Square; Fort Worth, Texas; Sundance Square Management • **Thin Flats**; Philadelphia, Pennsylvania; Onion Flats • Vancouver Convention Centre West; Vancouver, British Columbia, Canada; BC Pavilion Corporation • The Visionaire; New York, New York; Albanese Organization & Starwood Capital

## 2010 EMEA

Citilab; Barcelona, Spain; Fundació per la promoció de la societat del coneixement • **Miasteczko Wilanów**; Warsaw, Poland; Prokom Investments/IN-VI Investment Environments • Mumuth Music Theatre; Graz, Austria; BIG Bundesimmobiliengesellschaft m.b.H • Palazzo Tornabuoni; Florence, Italy; Kitebrook Partners/R.D.M. Real Estate Development

## 2010 Asia Pacific

Dragon Lake Bridge Park; Bengbu, China; Xincheng Comprehensive Development Zone Bengbu • Greenbelt 5; Makati City, Philippines; Ayala Land, Inc. • Newton Suites; Singapore; UOL Group Ltd. • **Rouse Hill Town Centre**; Rouse Hill, Australia; The GPT Group • **The Southern Ridges**; Singapore; Urban Redevelopment Authority of Singapore

**Project names in red indicate ULI Heritage Award winners.**
**Project names in blue indicate ULI Global Award for Excellence winners.**

# 2010 ULI GLOBAL AWARDS FOR EXCELLENCE

## THE GLOBAL AWARDS JURY

The chairman of ULI appoints the jury, which consists of five distinguished land use development and design practitioners. The chair of ULI's Policy and Practice Committee serves as the jury's chair. The other members are the chairs—or designees—of the three regional juries for Awards for Excellence and an at-large appointee. The 2010 Global Awards jury comprised the following members:

**Joe Brown,** Jury Chair, *group chief executive, AECOM, San Francisco, California*
**Marty Jones,** *president and CEO, MassDevelopment, Boston, Massachusetts*
**Nicholas Brooke,** *chairman, Professional Property Services Ltd., Hong Kong, China*
**Ian D. Hawksworth,** *managing director, Capital & Counties, London, United Kingdom*
**Richard Gollis,** *principal, The Concord Group, Newport Beach, California*

The ULI Global Awards for Excellence recognize projects that provide the best cross-regional lessons in land use practices. Up to five global winners may be named each year—chosen from among the year's 20 winners in the Americas, EMEA, and Asia Pacific—by a select jury of international members.

In 2010, there were five global winners, which were announced October 15 at the ULI Fall Meeting in Washington, D.C.

Because the Global Awards jury considers only projects that have been judged to have met ULI's criteria for an Award for Excellence, the jury bases its award determination on how projects meet the following standards:

- Establishing innovative concepts or standards for development that can be emulated around the world;
- Showing strong urban design qualities;
- Responding to the context of the surrounding environment;
- Exemplifying, where applicable, universally desirable principles of development, such as sustainability, environmental responsibility, pedestrian-friendly design, smart growth practices, and development around transit; and
- Demonstrating relevance to the present and future needs of the community in which they are located.

## Winners of the 2010 Global Awards for Excellence

### The Americas

**L.A. LIVE**
Los Angeles, California
**Owner:** AEG

**Jury Statement:** L.A. LIVE, anchored by the STAPLES Center and featuring 5 million square feet of entertainment, hospitality, and office uses, has transformed a stretch of underused land in downtown Los Angeles into a vibrant, 24-hour entertainment district and stimulated the development of more than 2,500 housing units, a grocery store, and dozens of restaurants and cafés in adjacent neighborhoods.

**Thin Flats**
Philadelphia, Pennsylvania
**Owner:** Onion Flats

**Jury Statement:** Certified LEED for Homes Platinum, Thin Flats is an eight-unit infill development in north Philadelphia that uses solar water heating, a green roof, and rainwater harvesting to reduce energy consumption by an estimated 50 percent. This prototype is now being scaled up for use in other cities, emerging as a development/design/build model that is replicable for infill sites across the country and even around the world.

## EMEA

**Miasteczko Wilanów**
Warsaw, Poland
**Owner/Developer:** Prokom Investments

**Jury Statement:** Miasteczko Wilanów—a pedestrian-oriented, architecturally rich new neighborhood in Warsaw—is a return to the urban morphology that was lost to the city in the war-torn 20th century. The 169-hectare mixed-use district is home to more than 20,000 residents and reestablishes sustainable planning and development practices in this rapidly expanding central European metropolis.

### Southern Ridges
Singapore
**Owner/Developer:** Urban Redevelopment Authority of Singapore

**Jury Statement:** The Southern Ridges is a nine-kilometer chain of open spaces that connects the rolling hills of three existing parks. The project, visited by a half-million people since its opening, creates a rare contiguous recreational space in densely populated Singapore.

## Asia Pacific

### Rouse Hill Town Centre
Rouse Hill, New South Wales, Australia
**Owner/Developer:** GPT Group

**Jury Statement:** Rouse Hill Town Centre, an ecologically conscious regional shopping center, features more than 210 retailers, 104 apartments, 2,800 square meters of office space, ten restaurants, and a cinema.